FOREWORD

by
David Attenborough

It was my great good fortune to have sailed on HMS *Endurance* for a short time during one of her ice patrols in the Antarctic. She was helping to maintain the British Antarctic Survey's bases on South Georgia, some of the other islands, and on the Antarctic continent itself. The Argentinians had not yet invaded the Falklands and it seemed a splendid and civilised thing that a vessel, which was nominally a warship, should be devoting her energies to assisting scientists in their study of one of the few parts of the world where man's influence is minimal and conditions so harsh that human beings need all the help and support they can get.

And what a marvellous world we saw. On one island we visited, a scientist had recorded a population of fourteen million chinstrap penguins. It hardly seemed possible. But when we got there, I could well believe the estimate was accurate. The birds were nesting and they stood as thick as a football crowd right round the volcanic island and up its flanks for several thousand feet until they were lost in the clouds. On South Georgia we found immense congregations of king penguins, solemnly conferring among themselves with their furry young, sea elephants lounging on the beaches, and albatrosses, pure white and with expressions of ineffable wisdom and patience, sitting on tall nest mounds that they and their forebears may have occupied for centuries.

We also, even at that time, heard talk of an illegal settlement by Argentinians of a small island away to the south, which seemed to have a military rather than a scientific purpose. But it seemed inconceivable that modern war could come to such a remote region, impossible that those few human beings who ventured into these harsh places should do anything other than help one another to survive.

Beautiful though the islands were, we were in no doubt that they were among the most inhospitable places on earth as far as man is concerned. For an afternoon the sun might shine so clearly and the sky be so blue, that you strip off your clothes and sun-bathe, but within a fraction of an hour, all that may change and gales of such ferocity blow up from nowhere that no boat can land on the rocks to rescue you, and no helicopter risk a landing for fear of being blown over. And then you learn how savage a country this is, how unforgiving it can be to people who are not totally prepared for the worst conditions at the shortest notice.

When we returned to Port Stanley in the Falklands we met Cindy Buxton and Annie Price. They, like us, were making a wild-life film and so we knew of one another's technical problems and aspirations. We listened with both admiration and amazement as they described their plans to spend several months alone at a remote bay on South Georgia. Their proposals sounded extraordinarily venturesome and had they come from others less experienced, they might have been put down as foolhardy. But Cindy and Annie knew perfectly well what risks they were running and what hardships they would inevitably have to endure. Both had spent two seasons in isolation before and both knew far more about what was involved than we did. And both were clearly so bewitched by the splendours of animal life there that those prospects daunted them not at all.

Over a year later, I was travelling in the Himalayas when I heard on my tiny portable radio the unbelievable news, to me, that Argentina had invaded the Falklands and that men, in that beautiful loneliness, were killing one another. It seemed bizarre in the extreme that Cindy and Annie, who had gone so far to escape from both the luxuries and the lunacies of civilisation, should have suddenly become caught up in this madness. Night after night, in the high valleys of Nepal, we listened to the news bulletins, trying anxiously to deduce from the guarded and cryptic accounts of the events on South Georgia what had happened to them both. It seemed a very long time indeed before one short sentence crackled over the ether to say that two British girls who were filming wildlife on the island had been 'found safe'. So I read the following pages of this book with the greatest curiosity, knowing full well that, as Cindy and Annie were involved, the story would be, to put it mildly, a lively one.

But, of course, this book is far more than the description of an

SURVIVAL: SOUTH ATLANTIC

SURVIVAL:
SOUTH ATLANTIC

Cindy Buxton
and Annie Price

Foreword by David Attenborough

GRANADA
London Toronto Sydney New York

Granada Publishing Limited
Frogmore, St Albans, Herts AL2 2NF
and
515 Madison Avenue, New York, NY 10022, USA
117 York Street, Sydney, NSW 2000, Australia
60 International Boulevard, Rexdale, Ontario R9W 6J2, Canada
61 Beach Road, Auckland, New Zealand

Published by Granada Publishing 1983

Copyright © Cindy Buxton 1983

British Library Cataloguing in Publication Data

Buxton, Cindy
  Survival.
  1. South Georgia (Island)—Description and travel
  —1951–
  I. Title   II. Price, Annie
  919.7'11'0924   F3031

ISBN 0–246–12087–8

Phototypeset by
Wyvern Typesetting Ltd, Bristol
Printed in Great Britain by
William Clowes (Beccles) Limited,
Beccles and London

Granada ®
Granada Publishing ®

incident in a crazy war. It is also an account of an encounter with wildlife in what is still, in spite of that war, one of the last unspoilt corners of our planet. If anyone can persuade the world at large, through words, films and photographs, of what a wonderland this is and how important that it should be preserved, it must surely be Cindy Buxton. It is a true pleasure to introduce and commend her book.

CONTENTS

TO MY BROTHERS AND SISTERS
MOPS, NICKY, TIM, ROO,
JAMIE AND VICKY
WITH LOVE

ACKNOWLEDGEMENTS

I would like to thank most sincerely the following people for all their kindness and help during my three years in the South Atlantic:

Jim Parker, Governor of the Falkland Islands 1976–9, and his wife Deirdre, who encouraged me in every way during my first year of filming

Rex and Mavis Hunt who gave me all their support during my second year in the Falklands

Ian and Maria Strange and Roddy and Lily Napier, joint owners of New Island, Rob and Lorraine McGill, owners of Carcass Island, and the late Len Hill, owner of Steeple Jason, who allowed Annie and me to live and work on their beautiful and unforgettable islands

Jack Sollis and the crew of MV *Forrest* who patiently transported us and one ton of equipment from one island to another for two years

The staff at Government House, in particular Nanny, Don and Keva

The Falkland Island Government Air Service who flew us for thousands of miles all round the islands

Griff and Gladys Evans, Iain and Hilda Stewart and all our other friends in the Falklands who gave us two wonderful years

The British Antarctic Survey for helping us to organise and set up camp at St Andrew's Bay, particularly Dr Richard Laws, the Director, Pete Witty, Base Commander at Grytviken, and Steve Martin, Deputy Base Commander, also Pete Stark, Tony North and Myles Plant, the three BAS personnel who joined Annie and myself at St Andrew's Bay just before the Argentinian invasion and put up with us for four long weeks

The Captain and crew of the RRS *John Biscoe* who took us south at the beginning of the season and the Captain and crew of the RRS *Bransfield* who were unable to take us north as planned at the end of the season owing to events beyond their control

Captain Nick Barker and the ship's company of HMS *Endurance* who went out of their way to help me with the filming on both Carcass Island and South Georgia: in particular I would like to thank them all for guarding us so well during the Argentinian occupation

Colin Willock, Mike Hay, Les Parry and all the Survival staff at Anglia Television in London, without whom this book would not have been possible

Mary Russell, a kind journalist, for helping me shape this book into its present form

Roger Schlesinger of Granada Publishing who gave me so much advice and encouragement

Finally, and most important of all, Annie Price, my assistant, who took most of the beautiful photographs in this book and who slaved away for countless hours over the typing and reading of the manuscript in the early days. Without her loyal support and help my three years in the South Atlantic would have been much more difficult.

CINDY BUXTON

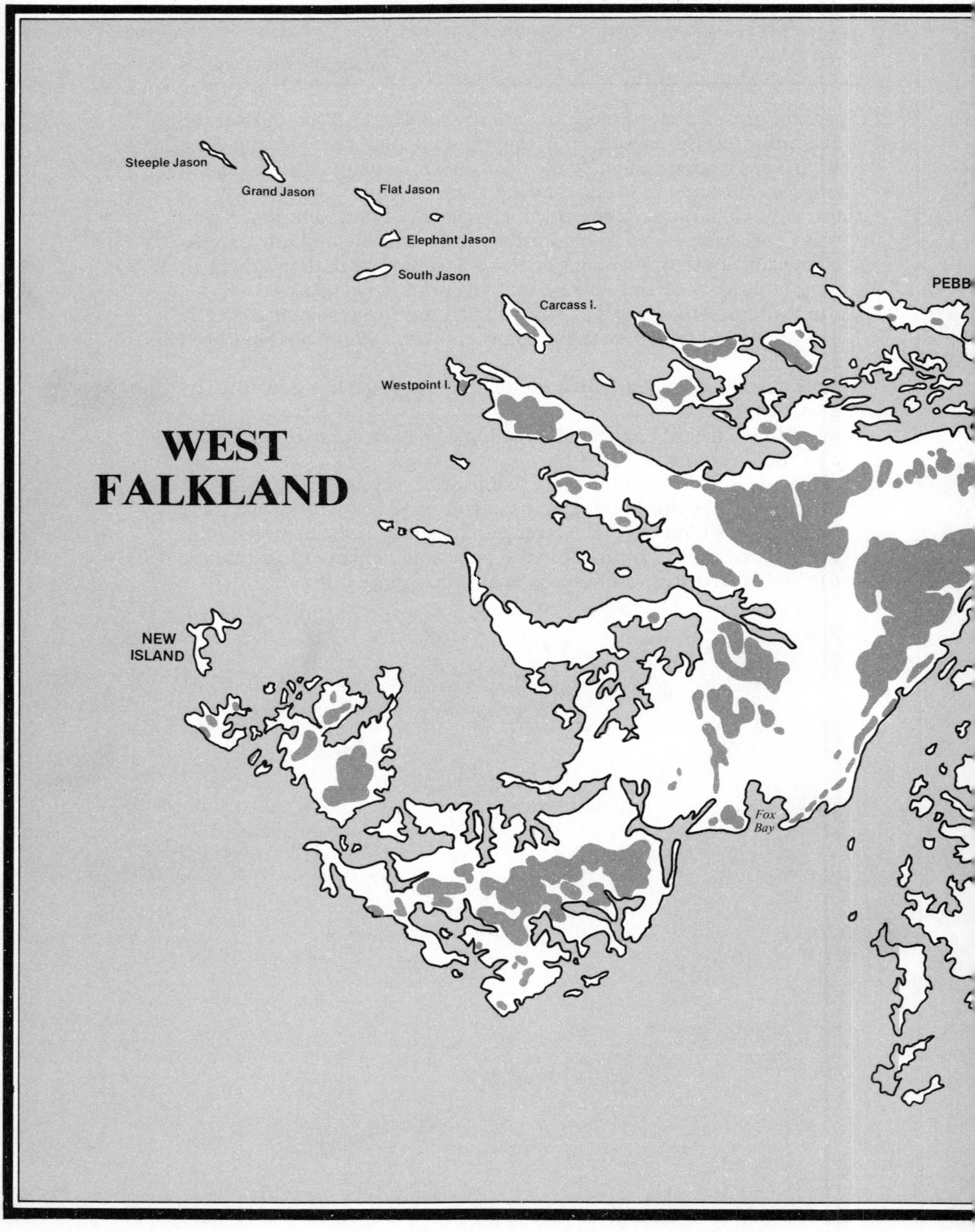

Steeple Jason

Grand Jason

Flat Jason

Elephant Jason

South Jason

Carcass I.

Westpoint I.

**WEST
FALKLAND**

NEW
ISLAND

Fox
Bay

PEBB

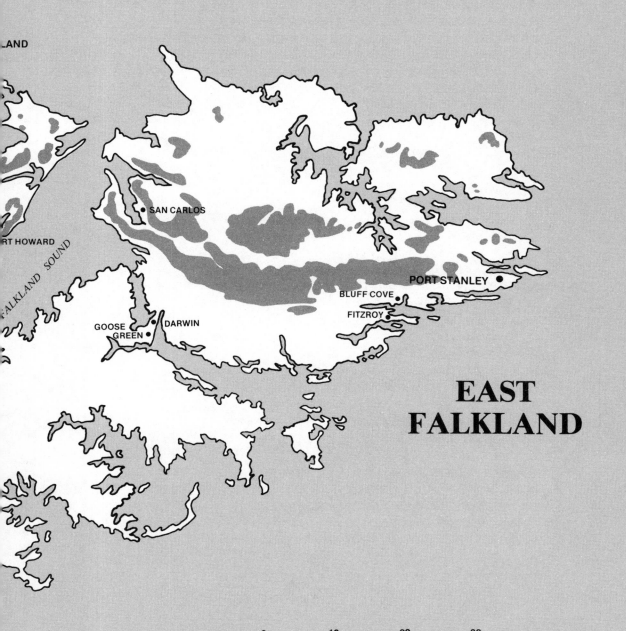

SOUTH
ATLANTIC OCEAN

EAST
FALKLAND

SAN CARLOS

PORT HOWARD

FALKLAND SOUND

PORT STANLEY

BLUFF COVE

FITZROY

GOOSE
GREEN

DARWIN

0   10   20   30 miles

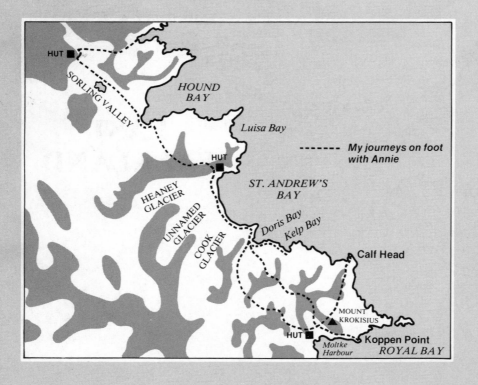

Bird I.

Schlieper Bay

KING HAAKON BAY

HUT ■

SORLING VALLEY

HOUND BAY

Luisa Bay

- - - - - - - *My journeys on foot with Annie*

HUT ■

ST. ANDREW'S BAY

HEANEY GLACIER

UNNAMED GLACIER

COOK GLACIER

Doris Bay

Kelp Bay

Calf Head

MOUNT KROKISIUS ▲

HUT ■

Moltke Harbour

Koppen Point

ROYAL BAY

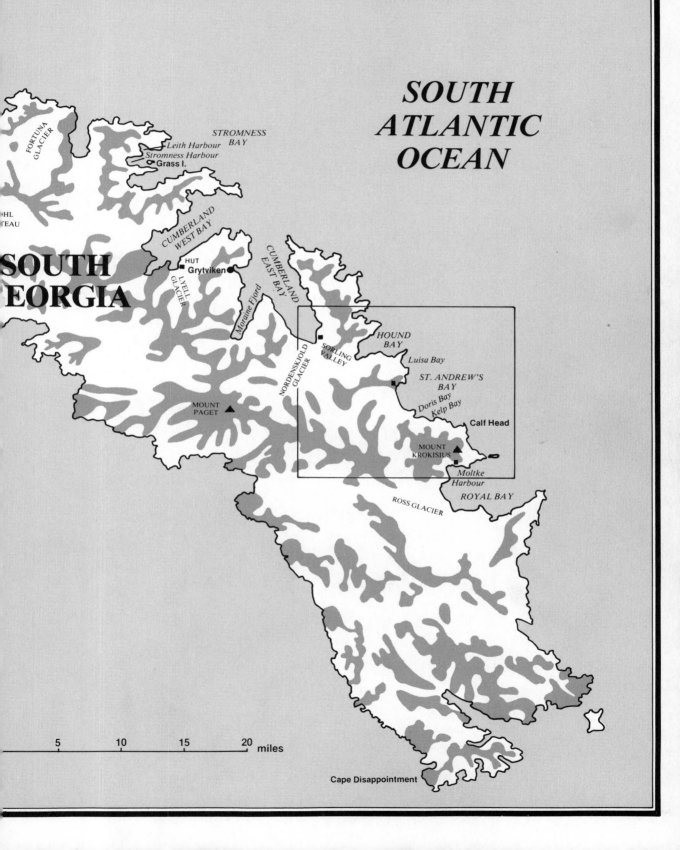

SOUTH
ATLANTIC
OCEAN

SOUTH
EORGIA

FORTUNA
GLACIER

STROMNESS
BAY

Leith Harbour
Stromness Harbour
Grass I.

HL
TEAU

CUMBERLAND
WEST BAY

CUMBERLAND
EAST BAY

HUT
Grytviken

LYELL
GLACIER

Moraine Fjord

NORDENSKJOLD GLACIER

SORLING
VALLEY

HOUND
BAY

Luisa Bay

ST. ANDREW'S
BAY

Doris Bay
Kelp Bay

Calf Head

MOUNT
PAGET

MOUNT
KROKISIUS

Moltke
Harbour

ROYAL BAY

ROSS GLACIER

5   10   15   20   miles

Cape Disappointment

PROLOGUE

THE RED ICEBERG

There was no doubt about it – the South Atlantic winter was setting in. The winds – high and bitterly cold – had dragged the temperature down well below freezing and the falls of snow had become more frequent. The sun, on the days we could see it, had dropped far down the sky. This meant that the power coming from my solar panel was getting steadily weaker. I had been using the panel to charge up the vital batteries for my radio – listening to the BBC World Service was virtually our only link with the outside world. I wasn't too concerned about the loss of solar energy as I did have a petrol generator but with the daylight hours gradually fading away and the temperature dropping, we were using more and more fuel for lighting and heating and it was the fuel supply that would be the first to go. We had, I reckoned, no more than a month's supply left.

There was no indication that Wednesday, 21 April, was going to be different from any other day in the previous three weeks we had spent in our hut on South Georgia under Argentinian occupation. The hut – 8 foot by 12 foot and barely big enough for Annie and myself – had also become home to three men from BAS, the British Antarctic Survey team, and for those three weeks the five of us had lived together in conditions so cramped that at times things became a little strained. That Wednesday afternoon, despite the howling wind and driving snow, Annie and I decided that we had to get out of the hut and go for a walk.

I looked at the thermometer. It was reading minus 5 degrees but once we ventured out into the biting wind, the wind-chill factor sent the temperature plummeting to minus 25 degrees. We struggled into our

Antarctic clothing – down-filled jackets, thermal gloves, balaclavas, thick felt padded snow boots and goggles to protect our eyes from the tiny particles of ice being blown off the glaciers. The gale hit us as soon as we opened the door but we wanted a breath of fresh air so much we almost welcomed it. We set out, heads down, almost uncontrollably running before the wind, making for Rocky Point where we hoped to catch a glimpse of a leopard seal. The driving snow and the salt spray caught us full on as we rounded the Point and I pulled down my snow goggles to give my eyes some protection. Something out on the horizon suddenly caught my eye – something solid in shape and I raised my goggles again to get a clearer look. Another iceberg? Only last week I had caused a certain amount of excitement when I had mistaken an iceberg for a ship. Today, the visibility was awful and the sudden gusts of snow made the object, whatever it was, disappear and then reappear. I stared at that iceberg, my eyes watering from the wind and stinging snow. It looked rather solid to me, maybe the colour wasn't quite right but there was something about it that made me think it wasn't just another iceberg and Annie felt the same.

We decided to go back to the hut to get the binoculars, struggling through the seventy-mph winds and shielding our noses and mouths from the stinging ice particles. Pete Stark, one of the BAS men, was in the hut and Annie decided to stay with the radio just in case anything came through. Pete joined me as, once more, I struggled to the gale-swept Rocky Point. We decided to climb up the steep tussock cliff where the young albatross chicks I had been patiently filming for seven months were now eagerly flapping their newly moulted wings, practising for the day when they would launch themselves into space and fly away. Up on the cliffs we could see a bit more of the strange iceberg.

We saw a clear patch of weather slowly working its way across the horizon and decided to wait for it to help us identify the object. We wriggled down into the tall, thick tussock grass, trying to get as much shelter as possible. For ten minutes, we sat waiting for this little patch of clear weather to move into position, our hands tucked under our arms, wriggling our toes to keep them warm, hunched up into tight balls thinking of log fires and hot baths. How long had it been since I had sunk into the luxury of a hot bath? So long ago I couldn't even remember.

As soon as the clear patch began to move onto the iceberg, Pete and I raised our binoculars and strained our eyes to pick out the distant

2

object. It came as a shock when we realised that it wasn't an iceberg but a ship – a real ship with men on board. But whose ship was it – Argentina's or the Royal Navy's? Now that we knew it was a ship, it was vital to discover whether it was friend or foe. If it was an Argentinian ship we had to race back to the hut and report it over the radio so that one of the BAS bases further south could hear us and pass the information on. We also knew that the Argentinians at Grytviken, a few miles north of us, could hear us. However, as they had made no attempt so far to reach us, we weren't too worried about them. If the ship turned out to be British then we would have to keep dumb, pretend we hadn't seen it and, at all costs, not tell the other field parties on the radio, thus giving vital information to listening Argentinians. Pete and I stared at the ship for the few brief moments that we were able to get a clear view of it. We could tell that the sea was rough because the ship kept disappearing down into troughs and then suddenly rearing up into full view as it rode up onto the crest of some huge wave. But we still couldn't be certain. Then the bow of the ship began to turn towards us – it was bringing its head into the wind – and as the bow rose up to ride over the crest of a wave, we saw the bright red hull, which was the giveaway. We knew of only one ship painted that colour – HMS *Endurance*, the Royal Navy's ice-patrol vessel and our guard ship. Pete and I looked at each other, huge grins on our faces which were now nearly blue with cold. We grabbed each other by the arm and said together, 'It's *Endurance*', and raced back to the hut.

Endurance meant something special to us. Its cheerful red colour was always a welcome sight, bringing, as it usually did, letters from home and through it we maintained contact with the world outside. We had last heard from Nick Barker, the Captain, three weeks ago. Since then – silence.

Even as we told Annie the news, our ears picked up, above the noise of the howling wind outside, the muffled engine of a helicopter. We strained anxiously to make out the sound and the familiar buzzing came as a relief. It was a helicopter from *Endurance* – a Wasp. Through the falling snow, the helicopter's single landing light beamed down on us like a glaring eye and we could just make out the windscreen wipers, working furiously to keep the pilot's vision clear. We quickly unfolded the Union Jack from around its pole, freeing it to give the pilot the correct wind direction. On a previous occasion, a visiting helicopter, miscalculating the wind direction, had turned over on landing. Now,

3

however, the Wasp hovered briefly near the flag, turned its nose into the wind and landed safely in the snow.

This was our first physical contact with the outside world since South Georgia had been invaded by the Argentinians three weeks before. From our isolated position fifteen miles south of Grytviken it had been difficult to know exactly what was going on.

Through Channel 13, the main radio frequency used by everyone on South Georgia, we had managed to keep in touch with all the field parties on the island, but since *Endurance* had been away and the unarmed BAS vessel, the *Bransfield*, had been recalled by London, we had been entirely on our own – never knowing if at any moment we might be taken prisoner. Now that *Endurance* had shown up again it looked as if something was about to happen. The helicopter from *Endurance* had come to land Chief Petty Officer Tommy Scott who was to put us in the picture and give us some advice on self-defence – just in case the Argentinians turned up.

We helped Tommy get his belongings into the two-man mountain tent and made sure that he had everything he needed, but we were delighted when, shortly, he returned to the hut laden with food from *Endurance*. There was bacon, a leg of lamb, a few steaks, a loaf of bread and even vegetables. Tommy was a delightful companion, small, a bit on the plump side, quiet and totally unflappable. While Annie got a delicious-smelling meal on the go – a welcome break from our usual diet of dehydrated meat granule stew – I poured out a drink for us all – sherry, in plastic mugs. Tommy, while he talked, dismantled his 9mm pistol, oiled, checked and reloaded it ready for use. With darkness falling and the wind howling outside, the cheerful smell of the cooking meal and the warm glow of the Tilley lamp were not enough to dispel the slight uneasiness and mounting excitement that very soon something was going to happen.

The following morning, Tommy taught Annie and me how to fire a pistol. Standing outside the hut while it was still snowing, he showed us how to slot the magazine full of bullets into the butt of the pistol, how to cock the weapon and how to stand when firing it. He warned that we should use the pistol if only one or two Argentinians showed up. If there were more than that, it would be pointless to fight them. We didn't fire any rounds as I was worried the penguins and other wildlife would get a fright and also it was just possible that the Argentinians at Grytviken might hear the shot. Tommy's instructions to us were to wait until the target was only thirty or forty feet away and then to aim at the chest and fire.

I couldn't help thinking how ridiculous this whole situation was. I had come down to the South Atlantic three years ago to make several films for ITV's wildlife programme 'Survival' and if all had gone according to plan, I would now be on my way back home with the films. Instead, I found myself unexpectedly enmeshed in a war.

1
PLANNING FOR SURVIVAL

It was Colin Willock, head of Anglia Television's Survival series, who first talked to me about the Falkland Islands. He had recently returned from a cruise to the Antarctic and on the way had been impressed by the huge penguin and albatross colonies on the Falklands. He showed me some of his slides of the wildlife there and told me what little history he knew. He thought it might be just my sort of place.

I read what I could about the Falklands and found out in July 1978 that the Governor, Jim Parker, happened to be in London with his wife on leave. The Survival office invited him over for lunch so that we could have a chat about the possibilities of filming. He was full of enthusiasm and eager for me to go to the Falklands and have a look around. So I agreed to fly out in November 1978 for one month and decide whether it would be worth moving myself and all my camera equipment there for a year or two.

I hadn't realised, until I made the journey to Stanley, the capital, just how far away the Falklands are. It took two and a half flying days to cover the eight thousand miles, with just one short stop in Buenos Aires. It was a cold, damp, grey and windy day when I stepped off the plane at Stanley Airport to be greeted by both the Immigration Officer and the Customs Officer, and it soon became clear that Jim Parker had talked on the local radio station about the filming I hoped to do. Everyone I met seemed to know who I was and they all wished me a pleasant stay.

I spent five days at Government House as a guest of Jim and Deirdre Parker. Jim, to my mind, was a typical Governor – rather large in every direction, with huge bushy, grey eyebrows and a deep voice. Deirdre was small with her long grey hair tied back in a bun. She was gentle, quiet and full of fun. The three of us got on well. Jim helped me in every manner possible to get the filming under way. I owe an enormous amount to both of them. Their driver/butler Don Bonner was another great source of help. He was always first with the intriguing details of the latest scandals. Every Government House should have a Don Bonner.

Port Stanley, compared to a town in England, is very small, almost a village. Built on a hillside, the terraced houses are much the same in size, each one with a quarter of an acre plot where the occupants grow vegetables and a few flowers. They are brightly painted little houses, with red tin roofs and smoke pouring out of the chimneys from the peat fires that are kept burning day and night. The main street runs along the bottom of the hill by the harbour where there is the only hotel, the only post office, the main shop and a few attractive private houses. Everything is small in Stanley and with a population of only one thousand there is no need for it to be any larger. Even the police station is small, with just one cell. During those first few days, I had long discussions with Jim Parker about the islands and the wildlife. Finally, I decided where I wanted to go and Government House kindly helped me to make the arrangements.

The Falkland Islands lie in the South Atlantic, 480 miles north-east of Cape Horn. They consist of two main islands with about two hundred smaller islands surrounding them. The land is hilly and bare of trees with an average temperature of 42°F. The total population before the Argentinian invasion was around 1,800 people. The main income of the Falklands is from the wool of the 600,000 sheep on the islands. Communication between the two main islands and the smaller islands is by radio telephone.

The first real effort to import sheep into the Falklands began in 1840. Sheep from Argentina were not hardy enough to withstand the cold, wet weather and many of them died. Eventually, stock was brought over from England and they proved much more successful. There are now about thirty-six farms on the Falklands. Those on the off-shore islands vary in size from 850 to 30,000 acres but, on the mainland, they can be as big as 307,000 acres.

From Stanley, I flew to New Island where I was particularly interested in doing some filming. Here, all along the shoreline, I found a mass of birds – geese, duck, plovers and oyster catchers. Everywhere I looked there were birds and I was keen to get the filming started.

New Island is jointly owned by Falkland Islanders Roddy Napier and

Ian Strange and it was Ian who agreed that I should rent the little A-frame hut that stood near his house. It needed one or two improvements but Ian assured me that they would all be done before I returned the following summer. Ian, in his mid-forties, tall and thin is an extremely good watercolour artist. When talking to you, he tends to give the impression of being far away elsewhere in his thoughts, but if you take the trouble to get to know him he is, in fact, the gentlest and kindest of men.

From New Island, I flew north to West Point Island. It was Roddy Napier who drew my attention to two uninhabited islands forty miles north of West Point – Steeple Jason and Grand Jason. I returned to Stanley and immediately began to make enquiries about getting to the Jason Islands. It was not going to be easy.

Back in London, I wrote my report for Survival and drew up a budget with a list of equipment and transport I would need. And, most important of all, for the first time in my life, I was going to need an assistant. 'If you want to get to Steeple Jason,' Jim Parker had said, 'I'll give you all the help I can but, remember, it's uninhabited so you can't go alone. Find yourself an assistant, otherwise I can't agree to your going.'

Finding someone was going to be difficult. Whoever came with me would have to stick it out for nine months as we would be totally cut off from the outside world. She would have to be prepared to work in cold, wet and, at times, dangerous conditions. Above all, she would have to take events as they came – although there was no way of knowing, at that point, that one of the events would turn out to be a full-scale war.

I had someone in mind but what would she think of the idea? Before asking her, however, I had another job to do. I travelled down to Gloucester to meet Len Hill, the owner of Steeple Jason. I needed his permission to film on the island. Len had bought both Jason islands for £5,000 in 1970. At that time they had sheep on them, but not being interested in farming Len had had the sheep slaughtered. The only inhabitants now were the wildlife.

By this time, all my equipment, including my car, had arrived back in England from Africa where, the previous season, I had been making a film about elephants. This all had to be repacked and sent on to its next destination – Iceland. I had another short film to make there on how the Icelandic farmer collects all the down from the nest of the eider duck and, having cleaned it, sells it for £150 a kilo. I managed to complete that film by the end of July and returned to England to learn that Survival had accepted my report and was prepared to give me the go-ahead. This meant I could start filming in the Falklands in September. There was no time to lose – I would have to find an assistant and quickly.

Annie Price and I had known each other for twenty years. We had gone to a convent boarding school together in Essex, and though we had not been in the same class we had known each other well – as rivals on the tennis court or when playing lacrosse. From there, I had gone to a domestic science college which I had enjoyed. After that, I went to a finishing school in Switzerland and returned to do the London season. But a month was about as much as I could take of that and I went on to Cambridge to do a secretarial course – and to learn to fly.

It was while I was at Cambridge that I received a telephone call from Des Bartlett who was going to the Galapagos Islands to make a wildlife film for Survival. Would I go with him and his wife and act as their assistant? The answer was most certainly yes. I learned a lot from Des and when I got back from the Galapagos I decided to go to Africa to try to make a film of my own for Survival. So, in 1971, I set out alone for Africa – and stayed there filming for eight years.

I had met up with Annie Price only once during that time. She, in the meantime, had had a variety of jobs – selling cosmetics and working as a personal assistant but, most important of all, she had spent five years as a photographer, specialising in child portraits. All a bit removed, perhaps, from the proposals I had to put to her: 'We'll be living in a small wooden hut on New Island,' I told her, 'and possibly in an old sheep shed on Steeple Jason. It will be difficult getting mail in or out. Our food will be tinned and dried and the weather will be cold and windy. And' – no point in beating about the bush – 'I can be extremely difficult to work with.' Surprisingly, she said yes. So that was it.

It was now a rush to get everything ready in time. Cameras, batteries, film, generator, heavy clothing, padded boots and all the other gear had to be packed into crates and air-freighted out to Stanley, via Argentina. Much to my surprise, the whole lot arrived in one piece three weeks later.

2

NEW ISLAND INITIATION

Once in Stanley, Annie and I rushed from one end of the town to the other getting everything organised – food, sleeping bags, petrol and oil for the generator, paraffin for the lamps and gas for cooking. We also had to hire a small rubber boat with an engine and buy some radio equipment. Because we were going to be totally cut off on Steeple Jason we had to be prepared for every eventuality. We had both paid £150 to insure ourselves against accidents but an insurance policy wasn't going to be much immediate use if some disaster actually happened. Before I set out on a trip like this, I always visit my dentist. In Africa I once had a tooth pulled out: instead of an anaesthetic, an African sat on my stomach while the 'dentist' took twenty minutes to extract the aching tooth – an experience I don't particularly want to repeat! My dentist in England usually gives me some dental filling and I have, on one occasion, filled my own tooth. On this trip, however, the filling was to be used in the end for repairs of a very different nature.

We paid a visit to the matron of the hospital at Port Stanley and she gave us a very useful crash course in survival. We were taught how to make splints, how to stitch up a wound and how to give an injection. Later, when we were about to set out for South Georgia, the hospital doctor went through the contents of the medical box with us as many of the items had twenty-letter unpronounceable names so that we weren't really sure if a bottle contained cough mixture or eye drops.

While making our final preparations for New Island, we stayed at Government House where Nanny, who had lived there for many years, took great delight in referring to us as her 'young girls'.

'How nice it is to hear the patter of tiny feet again,' she would say, making us laugh as both of us are over thirty. I remember going into the kitchen one evening, shortly before dinner, and finding Nanny stirring the soup – with a cigarette dangling out of her mouth. We started talking and I watched in amazement, as a large column of ash fell into the soup. Unperturbed, Nanny gaily stirred it in. I have never been quite sure whether she even noticed. The soup that evening was quite delicious and Annie and I always referred to all the soups at Government House as 'fag ash soup'.

This was the first leg of the trip and Annie was behaving a little timidly. No doubt, it was all a bit overwhelming for her. Anyway, Jim Parker decided she needed a programme of morale boosting and every day he would make her repeat after him, 'I am Annie and I am great. Nobody could do anything around here without me.'

During our second year filming on the Falklands Jim and Deirdre Parker completed their three years' service and left, to be replaced by the new Governor – Rex Hunt and his wife Mavis.

Rex, quite different from Jim, is small and very informal, wanting everyone to pop into Government House whenever they felt like it. There were numerous parties which went on long into the night and at first the islanders were a little mystified by this sudden informality. Rex is keen on wildlife and photography and gave me as much support as I had received from the Parkers.

He especially enjoyed snooker and whenever we stayed with the Hunts, we always ended up playing until some ungodly hour in the morning. We also played a lot of squash together, exhausting each other within an hour or two.

It was Jim Parker, however, who gave us all the help in the early stages and organised everything we needed for that first trip.

Departure day finally arrived and we loaded all our equipment onto MV *Forrest*. MV *Forrest* belongs to the Falkland Islands Government and was leased out to the Ministry of Defence for use by the Royal Marines. It was later commandeered by the Argentinians. There are no sleeping quarters for women on the *Forrest*, so we flew direct to West Point Island to await the *Forrest* there. Stepping out of the Beaver float plane into the little rowing boat where Roddy Napier and I were waiting, Annie's foot slipped on the wet plane float and she fell into the icy water. As she fell, she grabbed me round the back of the neck, almost pulling me out of the boat, and causing the whole craft to tilt dangerously over to one side. Roddy, trying to keep the balance, leant right over on the other side while the pilot and I hauled Annie out of the water.

We rowed to the landing stage where I proudly presented my new assistant, Annie, who was now soaking wet and shivering from her icy dip, her hair festooned with seaweed.

We spent the night on West Point Island and joined the *Forrest* the following day. Fifteen-foot waves broke over the ship and we both turned a pale shade of green during the four miserable hours it took to reach New Island, where we had to unpack in the pouring rain. Ian Strange was away so the island was completely deserted. The crew of the *Forrest* helped us unload our equipment and carry it up from the boat. Shivering, wet and still feeling the effects of our sea journey, I was longing to get settled into the little hut that was to be our home. Shelter from the rain, a change of clothes and a hot cup of tea would revive us, I knew, but my heart sank when I opened the door. None of the things which Ian promised to do last year had been done. The floor was covered with sacks of flour and sugar and general junk – and the window wouldn't open. Still, it wasn't the end of the world and the Royal Marines from the Stanley Garrison who were on board *Forrest* set to work lighting the gas fire, turning on the water supply and setting up my radio aerial before sailing away and leaving us on our own.

It took us several days to sort out camp. Having removed all the things we found in the hut and stored them safely in a shed, we set about scrubbing it out before unpacking our equipment. It was quite a nice little hut – ten foot square – with two beds, a table, two chairs, a gas fire, running water heated by gas and a chemical loo. There was one large window facing north which, in the southern hemisphere, is the sunny side and this made the hut terribly hot on sunny days but, without insulation, it was bitterly cold on wet days, with the little gas fire making no difference. The heat went straight out through the thin roof. The window still wouldn't open, no matter how hard we tried, which meant that, at night, we had to leave the door open to get some air. More than once we woke to find a two-foot snowdrift in the middle of the room. However, it was dry and well built and was going to be our home for the next six months.

Wherever I start a trip, I always have to spend some time making my new home as comfortable as possible – not always an easy task but after a day's filming in the rain or snow, followed by a five- or six-mile walk back to base carrying my equipment on my back, I find I perk up if I have a few basic comforts to come home to, and being warm and dry are at the top of my list. Annie carries home-making further than I do and her first task is to prop up some family photographs which always make me feel guilty as I haven't any of *my* family. I do, however, now travel with

13

a hot-water bottle though until I saw Annie's it had never crossed my mind to get one. Annie's other travelling bottle is a brandy flask which she maintains is for her queasy stomach. I don't drink much myself although we've always managed to have a glass – plastic mug, really – of sherry each evening wherever we've happened to be. There was to be one terrifying occasion, though, on South Georgia, when I was very glad indeed to accept Annie's offer of a drink from her flask – the first time I had ever tasted brandy.

During that first week, the sun shone every day but the winds blew, sometimes up to sixty miles an hour. The black-browed albatross had already arrived at the colony at the top of the hill behind the hut. They were busy building up their tall mud nests and going through their courtship display and mating. Down at the south end of the island, the gentoo penguins had also arrived and were busy building their simple nests of stones and grass, mating and calling to each other all the time. We put up a small tent near their colony so that if it suddenly turned nasty with rain or snow when we were filming them, we would have somewhere to take shelter.

Annie had never put up a tent before and although willing to try anything once, almost managed to strangle herself in all the guy ropes as the tent tried to take off in the strong wind. That first week was sheer hell. We had to carry all our heavy camera equipment up and down the hills, battling against the wind. Our legs and backs hated every moment of it all until they finally got used to it. But it was the wind that really tired us out. Walking into a sixty-mph wind, carrying thirty pounds on our backs, was no fun. The force of the wind literally drove the breath out of us, leaving us gasping like fish out of water. It could stop us in our tracks and even, on occasion, force us back again. Climbing over the rocks was slow and difficult work as we were easily caught off balance. The bitter cold left our hands, feet and face numb and after several hours of sitting with the birds we would develop violent shivering attacks. By the end of each day we were utterly exhausted.

Annie found it all very difficult to start with. The first fence she had to climb over she split her trousers. She cut herself so often with her new penknife that we ran out of sticking plaster in the first week and I had to take the penknife away from her.

During those first few weeks on New Island, she seemed to fall over every rock and clump of grass that she could find but as the weeks went by she gradually got the hang of it and became much more nimble on her feet. Every Sunday, we would take the morning off to wash our hair and clothes. The first time we hung out the clothes to dry we found

LEFT   Jim and Deirdre Parker outside Government House taking the Salute on Battle Day

BELOW   The staff of Government House and myself

ABOVE With Maria Strange on New Island

LEFT The hut we lived in on New Island

OPPOSITE Filming on New Island

ABOVE Our shed on
Steeple Jason
RIGHT With the
radio

OPPOSITE PAGE

ABOVE An aerial
view of Steeple Jason
BELOW LEFT Annie
cooking supper
inside our shed
BELOW RIGHT Pouring
stored rain water
into the drum to
heat it for washing

Part of the vast black-browed albatross and rockhopper penguin colony on
Steeple Jason

OPPOSITE ABOVE A pair of black-browed albatross at their nest with their three-week-old
chick, surrounded by rockhoppers
OPPOSITE BELOW Beside some black-browed albatross nests

ABOVE The pink pool on Steeple Jason. I sent a sample of the water back to Britain for analysis and was told that the colouring was due to the high concentration of krill in the guano

LEFT Sitting on a huge tripot which was used by the sealers to boil down penguins for their oil

ABOVE   A great skua with its chick

RIGHT   A striated caracara with a dead rockhopper chick in its beak which it will feed to its young

A pair of upland geese with chicks on the shoreline

LEFT   A pair of rockhoppers with their first egg

BELOW LEFT
A rockhopper attempting to give shelter and warmth to its over-sized chick

OPPOSITE ABOVE   A downy rockhopper chick being fed by one of its parents

OPPOSITE BELOW
A partially moulted rockhopper chick with its parents

most of them missing after half an hour. The wind had blown them away and we had to go over the island collecting missing socks and bras that had been blown into gorse bushes, goose droppings and ditches or had been caught on old barbed-wire fences. We soon learnt that one pair of pants required three pegs.

Ian Strange and his wife, Maria, turned up after a month to spend the summer in their little house not far from our hut. Every evening, we would go over to have supper with them and the occasional bath. We got on well together and had countless hysterical evenings playing games and telling stories. They loved to hear some of my stories about my eight years in Africa. One evening, Annie decided to show Ian and Maria how to do headstands. When she was in the middle of one of them, Ian got up and placed a jug of water on her bottom so that if she moved the whole thing would have gone all over her. He wouldn't allow either of us to rescue her for quite some time.

One day when I was filming near Ian's house, I watched him climb up on to the roof and try to push a chimney brush down the chimney. No matter how hard he huffed and puffed he could not get the brush to fit. The chimney, apparently, was half blocked with soot and this was causing the paraffin stove to smell and smoke. I yelled up to Ian that what he needed was a pair of scissors to trim the brush. I'd meant it as a joke but to my surprise he called back: 'Good thinking, Cindy', and climbed down off the roof to get a pair of Maria's best scissors. I giggled to myself and got on with my filming. A few minutes later the wind coming from Ian's direction brought one or two prize swear words. The chimney brush had got well and truly stuck halfway down the chimney. Leaving my camera, I climbed up on to the roof of the house to see if I could help in any way. The two of us were heaving on the brush trying to get it to move in one direction or another when a very powerful gust of wind nearly blew us both off the roof. I turned round and was just in time to see my tripod, with the camera on top, keel over as another gust of wind caught it, sending the camera flying. I leapt down off the roof and was greatly relieved to find the whole thing had fallen onto soft ground and no damage had been done.

Having cleaned up the camera and laid it safely on the ground, I went back to help Ian. He asked me to go into the house and assist Maria. I found her in the kitchen, shirt sleeves rolled up, with one arm up the flue of the stove, trying to push the brush back up again. Her hair, face, neck and arms were covered in soot. I sighed, rolled up my shirt sleeves and joined in. Half an hour later we managed to free the brush.

During the bad days on New Island, when it wasn't possible to film, Annie and I would stay in the hut, cleaning and repairing the equipment, charging up the batteries, writing up filming notes, reading or playing some kind of game – cards perhaps, or backgammon. We would also tune in the radio to the frequency used by everyone on the islands to call up Stanley, just to keep up with the local news. I'll never forget the day when the Stanley radio operator called up one of the islands to announce the arrival of a telegram from England. 'Hang on a minute, don't read it out yet,' called the recipient, 'I've got some cakes in the oven and I want to get them out in case they burn.' We practically fell off our chairs laughing.

Sometimes we would tune into the BBC World Service for events like the Grand National or the Boat Race – Annie yelling for Oxford and me for Cambridge. Unfortunately, we often got the time difference between London and the Falklands in a muddle and missed whatever we wanted to listen to, sometimes by hours. In the evenings we would listen to the local Falklands Island radio station transmitting from Stanley. That way we got news from Britain as well as the local news, plays, radio games and music. The announcers had their own unique way of introducing things. Unlike the precision timing of the BBC, they would announce: 'Sports Round-Up will be at about 7.45 and we'll have the news around eight.' One evening, the announcer was reading out a list of things for sale when suddenly he stopped. There was a long silence and then he came back again. 'I'm so sorry, I'm afraid I can't pronounce this next word so we'll just have to skip it.'

During the months of January, February and March, New Island was covered with wild mushrooms which we would pick on our way back to the hut. They were almost our only form of fresh food and we loved eating them. The other food we were able to collect were mussels which grew in large numbers in the sheltered bays along the east coast of New Island. They were huge, beautiful mussels and many evenings we would go out and collect a bucketful for supper. One calm, sunny evening while we were making our way along the white sandy beach, we heard a strange high-pitched squeaking noise. It appeared to be coming from further along the beach, so we went to investigate. To our amazement, we found thousands of squid deliberately beaching themselves during a falling tide. They occasionally squirted out powerful jets of water and wriggled about until, five or six minutes later, all movement stopped and they died. No single reason has yet been found for this phenomenon. I was able to film all this and I hung around for a few days as I knew that many birds would soon swoop down to the beach to feed off the easy meal. Gulls, giant petrels, albatross, seals, striated caracaras and the skuas all arrived for the mammoth feed and in no time had cleaned up the beach.

During the summer months Ian and Maria catered for tourists. I was not keen on the tourists as they always seemed to get in my way and want to look at my camera equipment. Ian and Maria would have groups ranging from one to ten people staying for a week or two at a time. When there were just a few tourists staying, life was reasonably sane but there were times when much larger groups turned up. Ian's house has four double rooms and only one bathroom, with Ian and Maria sleeping in the attic. The queue for the bathroom in the mornings and evenings was ridiculous. People would dash in and out of the house with cameras and binoculars flying and ten pairs of boots would bring half the island into the house when they returned. Poor Maria would slave away from dawn to dusk over the paraffin stove trying to feed them all and would, quite understandably, blow a gasket should any of them dare to complain or get in her way. Annie and I would stay firmly in our hut or go to the other end of the island to film while all this was going on.

Ironically, it was a group of tourists who unwittingly caused a major row between the two of us. Our day usually began at about six a.m. Filming was often cut short by bad weather and when we got a good day I liked to make an early start. One particular morning, I was especially anxious to get away as we had a long walk to the colony. Leaving Annie to carry her own stills equipment and my tripod, I loaded the heavy camera, magazine, cables, lenses and transistor box into my rucksack. The heavy twenty-seven-volt battery I have to use for slow-motion filming is specially shaped to be carried on the hip but we had a three-mile walk ahead of us and after a while I knew we would have to share the weight. I walked on ahead, struggling against the wind which whistled past my face, but after a mile I had to stop to put down my load – and wait for Annie. I could see her well behind, talking to some of the tourists, German I think they were. I called to her to hurry up but the wind carried my voice away. By now it was 8.30 and we still had another two miles to go. I got my load up onto my back again, settled the battery on my hip which, by now, was feeling crushed under the weight and started my slow progress into the wind. At the next stop, my fingers were so numb I could hardly undo the carrying straps of the battery. The whole point of having an assistant was the extra pair of hands to help with this sort of thing, but there was no sign of Annie. I let the battery thud down onto the ground beside me and climbed up onto a mound to get a better view. A good half hour's walk away, I could see Annie struggling along slowly. Bad weather had left me about three days behind with my film schedule and now I was being held up again, by Annie. I was beside myself with frustration and fury as I watched her painfully slow progress and, as soon as she was within shouting distance, I yelled at her. That was a mistake – she stopped.

'Where the hell have you been?' I shouted.

'Talking to those German tourists,' she called back. 'They wanted to know what we were filming.'

'And you told them, I suppose?'

'Of course. It would have been rude – in the middle of nowhere – to walk past a group of people and not stop to say hello.'

It's not very easy to have a shouting match in a forty-mph gale and, angry as I was, I had to pick up my things and stamp off as best I could. However, it wasn't Annie's policy to be co-operative that day and though she followed me, she did so very, very slowly. Suddenly I snapped. Putting down all my equipment, I turned round to face her.

'Come here.'

Annie stopped. 'Don't you tell me what to do.'

'Come here, *now*!'

'No, I won't,' she yelled, 'and you can stop giving me orders – we're not in the army.'

'Right, Annie. That's it. You come here and do as I tell you. You knew what you were letting yourself in for when you agreed to come here – you can't back down now. Come *here*!'

'No, I'm not your bloody dog.'

We both glared at each other, rigid with anger. After a few moments, Annie silently and somewhat dejectedly crossed the tussock grass till she was standing in front of me and then we had the real row – no holds barred.

I don't think we spoke to each other much for the rest of that day. I'd never had to give anyone orders before and I had to learn how to do it with grace. Annie, too, I knew, found it difficult to draw the line between boss and friend.

Poor Annie took some time to adjust but she had been warned. She gradually learned to know when it was wiser to stay out of my way. One of her means of defence was to keep behind me – but not too far behind – when we were out tramping in the snow or rain. She also seemed to know when not to talk and could withdraw into a book and leave me to myself. She must be the most long-suffering assistant around.

In a way, having a monumental row like that one right at the beginning of the trip was the best thing that could have happened – we never had another one and frequently had a laugh about it.

3

CHRISTMAS ON STEEPLE JASON

I had decided to divide my first filming season between Steeple Jason and New Island. Steeple Jason, the most northerly of the Falkland Islands, is difficult to reach – and even more difficult to land on. It has no natural harbour and the coastline is virtually straight, with huge jagged rocks protecting the shore. There are no sandy beaches.

When Jack Sollis, Captain of the MV *Forrest*, turned up again after a month to collect us from New Island, he put it to me bluntly: 'We'll take you up there and see what the weather's like but I have to warn you, if conditions aren't good, I'm not going in. It'd be too dangerous. I'll land you on Grand Jason instead.'

The trouble was, I didn't *want* to go to Grand Jason. We'd made our preparations, loaded about a ton of equipment onto *Forrest* and Steeple Jason was where I had to go, weather permitting, of course. Jack, however, was only prepared to have a go providing the wind was right and there was no swell. We had with us enough food to last us the two months we expected to be there. Our plan to spend some time living on an uninhabited island had caught the imagination of everyone on the Falklands and the whole adventure was regarded with increasing excitement. Steeple is looked upon by the Islanders as a special island with a certain amount of mystery surrounding it. No one had ever lived there for any length of time and little was known of it except that the wildlife was thought to be spectacular. The only thing that was known for sure was that the winds could reach a hundred mph. When Steeple had about eight hundred sheep on it five or six men would sail over once a year from one of the other islands to shear the sheep and bale the wool – and then, after several days, they would leave again for another twelve months. The men lived in a small shed with wooden bunks next to the bigger shearing shed. The shearing shed was destroyed by gales in 1960 and replaced by a sturdier one. Another storm demolished the small living shed, and the cast iron stove which had been in it was found fifty yards down the beach. All that is left now is twisted metal and rotten floorboards. The shoreline is littered with the evidence of many shipwrecks including the keel of what was once a large sailing ship. After all the sheep on the island were slaughtered, both Steeple and Grand Jason were left undisturbed and in fact, until we went there, no one was really sure whether the apparently spectacular wildlife had flourished or not.

As we approached Steeple Jason, everything seemed set for landing but I watched Jack Sollis's face anxiously. The final decision would have to be his. If he said no, then the whole focus of this filming season would have been lost.

'Right,' said Jack, 'we'll go in but I won't be able to drop anchor. The sea-bed here falls right away to over a hundred fathoms. We'll have to unload while we're still moving.'

No wonder he was anxious there should be no swell – unloading took us three hours. While *Forrest* gently cruised up and down the coastline, our equipment was lowered into one of the rubber boats which sped away to land on the rocky shore, some fifty yards from the old shearing shed. Annie and I stayed on board making quite sure that all our things had been off-loaded, then we went ashore ourselves.

A couple of members of the crew, together with some Royal Marines from the garrison at Stanley, helped us set up the radio aerial. We had been able to have the use of a large tent belonging to the Marines and this we fixed up *inside* the shed, securing the guy-ropes to the slatted floor and the beams. When all was ready, *Forrest* blew her foghorn several times, turned her back on us and steamed away. We watched her disappear round the south-east end of the island, knowing we were now on our own for the next few months. I was so thrilled to be on Steeple Jason at last that I could hardly wait to get to know the island. However, first things first.

As I have already said, to work well over a long period, camp has to be organised, warm and as clean and tidy as possible. We began the job of turning the draughty, dirty shearing shed into a cosy home. The tent was already up so we hunted around and found some old baling sacks in a corner. These we split and laid flat on the floor in the tent to stop the howling draught coming up through the floorboards. It took us two days of brushing and sweeping to clear the shed. Sheep's wool and dust flew everywhere and, at one point, Annie stopped for a rest. 'I think,' she said, 'I'll make a cup of tea. I have got so much lust in my dungs I don't know what to do.' We were almost too exhausted to laugh.

Into the tent we put our camp beds, sleeping bags, suitcases, a table and two chairs. In the evenings, having pulled the front flap of the tent down, we would light the Tilley lamp and hang it up and wait while it gradually warmed the tent, and calmed our violent shivering attacks. Annie was now in complete charge of the kitchen area which consisted of a long baling table covered with old sacks. We placed all the tinned and dried food on the table and although we had to watch out for mice, there were luckily no rats on Steeple Jason. We put drinking water in jerry cans under the table and our two giant gas cylinders stood nearby. All my camera cases and film were pushed against one of the walls near the tent. I banged in several nails to hang up coats, hats and binoculars and taped up a large map of Steeple Jason on one of the walls. In another section of the shed, I set up all the radio and electrical equipment. One of the few luxuries I allowed myself was a good radio with a digital read-out. This meant I could tune in immediately to the exact frequency I wanted without having to waste time fiddling with the tuning knobs. We also had a Government-owned radio, known locally as the Black Box. The Black Box was the main radio-telephone link, which all the islanders used to communicate with each other and Stanley. My own little two-meter set, which was not an official radio, had a far smaller range and I used it purely for private conversations between friends on nearby islands. Unfortunately, the Black Box was a little temperamental and although it usually transmitted all right, it often refused to receive. So, when holding a conversation with Stanley, I would talk through the Black Box but take the replies via my little transistor which I had tuned in to the right frequency. Usually in the evenings someone would call me up on the two-meter set – Sedge Island or Carcass Island were the regular ones – to tell me if there were any messages or not. If there were, I would call up Stanley on the Black Box the following morning.

When a strong wind was blowing, we soon found that the twisted ruins of the old shed battered persistently against our own shed and with the use of some strong-looking poles which we found lying around we managed to lever the old shed off our own.

We also inspected the rainwater tank and found it needed some repairs. There was a large four-hundred-gallon tank next to the shed, full of water which had been brought there by an ingenious system of guttering. The water ran down along the guttering into a wooden box, down through a pipe and finally went into the tank. Unfortunately, the wooden box was full of muck and leaked like a sieve. My own ingenuity, however, did not fail me. I got hold of an old biscuit tin and nailed it to the bottom of the wooden box. Then I drilled a hole in the tin directly over the pipe leading into the tank. This system worked extremely well and during our time on Steeple the water level in the tank never dropped lower than half.

Lamps and paraffin and various battery chargers were kept near the radio, but I built a wooden shelter for my generator about thirty yards away from the shed to reduce the noise. Most evenings, I would run the generator for about an hour to charge up all the batteries.

One other important bit of furniture in the shed was the chemical loo. We put a lot of thought into finding the best position for it and in the end came up with a most satisfactory solution. We found that if we placed it in line with the back door of the shed we could sit and look out, down into a shallow Magellan penguin burrow where a bird was sitting on her two white eggs. We spent many happy hours on the loo, observing the bird, though I always resisted the urge to bring my camera in as well.

Once we had thoroughly cleaned the shed and either burned or buried the rubbish, we at last started out to explore the island. Whenever we left the shed, we took our cameras with us, regardless of the weather. As well as assisting me, it was Annie's job to do all the still photography. We spent two days walking round the island – first to the north-west end and on the second day going to the south-east point. Steeple Jason is roughly 2,500 acres in size, with a sharp thousand-foot ridge running down the backbone of the island. The land on the west side slopes steeply to the sea, although on the other side the incline is more gradual, the slope down to the sea covering a distance of about half a mile. The central ridge is broken half way down the island where there is a thin strip of land only a few hundred yards wide and completely flat. This acts as a diagonal divide between north-west and south-east. Our shed was situated about fifty yards from the sea on the east side, just under the south-east peaks which were supposed to give us protection from the strong westerly winds.

That first day, on our seven-hour walk round the north-west end, we came across Magellan penguins nesting in their burrows all over the island and we also discovered they were very tame and approachable. Wandering around the penguins were thousands of upland geese with their chicks. About a mile from our shed on the east side of the island, we found exactly what we were looking for – a large group of nesting gentoo penguins, some of them with chicks that had just hatched. We sat down on the ground to watch and were amazed when about a hundred of them got up from their colony and came to within three feet of us to stand and stare. Any sudden movement would send them all scattering back to the colony but after a few minutes they would slowly return to sit down and stare again. They were full of curiosity. A mile further along the east coast we found another, even larger gentoo colony, this time amongst the tussock grass. Among the tussock clumps lurked the striated caracaras and the skuas, birds which preyed on the gentoos should they, even for a minute, fail to guard their eggs or chicks. The striated caracara is known locally as Johnny Rook.

The rich, tall tussock grass grows everywhere and is a bit like the marram grass reeds which grow among sand dunes in Britain. Some of the penguins use it to line their nests and it can be eaten – as we found out later.

Having struggled through the tussock grass and out the other side, we came across a small sea-lion colony down on the rocks by the sea. I was particularly pleased about this find because until then I had virtually no film of any of the seals found on the Falklands. We decided to pitch a tent nearby using the tussock grass as shelter so that when filming in this area we had some protection during the day, if we needed it. When we finally reached the north-west end of the island, we found our way barred by very tall, dense clumps of tussock grass and we decided therefore to climb halfway up the ridge to see if there was anything interesting on the other side. What we saw left us gasping.

Stretched out in a swath a hundred yards wide along the north-west coast and reaching into the distance was one huge continuous mass of black-browed albatross and rockhopper penguins, all packed tightly together. The single colony was approximately six miles long – a breathtaking sight. Now we had no choice. We would *have* to get through the tussock grass and into the colony. We climbed down from the ridge and began forcing our way through the grass until the deafening noise told us we were getting near the colony. We were unable to hear each other above the din. The sky above us was filled with albatross as we came onto a seething mass of birds, all screeching at the same time. Standing downwind, the powerful ammonia smell choked us and we had to turn away. Stepping over the penguins and round the tall mud nests of the albatross, we made our way back round the colony, our progress going unnoticed as long as we were careful and moved slowly.

On our tour of the south-east end of the island we found the usual

Magellan penguins nesting in their burrows, as well as large groups of upland geese. After a three-hour walk, we came across an area of tussock grass that had been totally destroyed by a fire which had burned the grass right down to the ground. Many years ago, when sealers made regular trips to Steeple they would set fire to the tussock to flush out the seals which they would then kill. The grass would smoulder for weeks, sometimes months, burning deep down into the soil and eventually rendering the whole area devoid of life. During the time we spent living on Steeple, we inspected these burnt-out areas and, even then, perhaps thirty years after the burning, we found only a few tiny new clumps struggling through the loose, black soil, desperately clinging to life. It was extremely difficult walking over these areas as the thin crust always gave way and we would sink knee-deep into the soil.

On our second day's walk, we found not only the other end of the vast albatross and rockhopper colony but also a couple of giant petrel colonies with a mass of skuas nesting all over the place. The giant petrels seemed nervous of us and one or two birds flew away when they saw us coming. This was the signal the striated caracaras, hovering overhead, were waiting for. In a flash, they descended from the sky and, tapping their beaks on the eggs temporarily abandoned by the petrels, they cracked them and began to eat the yolk. From then on, we were very much more careful of the way in which we approached the petrels. The petrel's habit of regurgitating foul-smelling liquid when threatened has earned it the local name of Stinker!

Because they defend their nesting areas so vigorously, the skuas proved to be a major problem for us. They would dive out of the sky like little spitfires and, swooping low over our heads, would deliberately lower their feet at the last moment to try to hit us, which they often did with considerable effect. One skua got Annie in the eye with its wing and we were forced to retreat into a clump of tussock until she recovered. Another skua hit me so hard on the chin that my knees buckled under me and although it didn't actually knock me out I felt pretty wobbly for a few minutes.

There were really far too many upland geese on Steeple and we frequently saw vicious territorial fights break out between the males. These fights would go on for a long time, only ending when one of the males became too exhausted to continue. One evening, standing disconsolately looking out at the rain which had been pouring down all day – keeping us from filming – I noticed a row about to break out between two upland geese, one of whom – the intruder – had brought along its mate and its family of five chicks. Despite the downpour, we grabbed the cameras and rushed out to film the dispute. The defending male flew at the intruding male and female, grabbed them by the neck and then hammered at them with his wings. If they managed to break away, he would chase them round and round the area. Then he would go for the chicks picking them up and throwing them in the air. The intruding pair, desperate to defend their young, would return and the defending male would, once again, turn on them beating them mercilessly with his wings. It wasn't long before a couple of striated caracaras arrived on the scene, ready to grab a young chick – which they did – when the parents' attention was elsewhere. It was a spectacular fight though with a miserable ending for the young, undefended chicks.

Our filming schedule was usually governed by the weather and, if everything was going smoothly, we would take Sunday morning off from work. We had brought with us an empty forty-gallon petrol drum which had already been split in half lengthways. On Sunday mornings, we would go down to the beach to collect driftwood to make a good fire near the shed. One half of the drum we filled with water and placed over the fire. With the aid of buckets, we would transfer the hot water into the other half of the drum which we had rested on a bracket. We would then strip, have a really good scrub and change into some clean clothes. What bliss after a week! We would drain the water and replace it with more hot water which we used to wash our hair. The final lot of water we used to scrub clean our dirty clothes and these were hung out over the old wire fencing near the shed – and clipped down very firmly with numerous pegs. If it rained, that was just too bad. We had been told that the striated caracaras, which were in much abundance on Steeple, had a great passion for stealing clothes and at the beginning we kept a sharp eye on the birds which lived near the shed. We soon found out that they weren't interested but I did take the precaution of warning Sedge and Carcass Island which were about forty miles south-east of us, that should they see any striated caracaras flying round with Marks and Spencer underpants clutched firmly in their claws they were ours – and we wanted them back.

Thieving birds, however, were the least of our problems on Steeple. The weather was our worst enemy and, on average, we saw the sun only fourteen days a month. It was often damp and bitterly cold. Out of the wind, the temperature might be 35–40°F, but up on the cliffs, with a fifty-mph wind, it was much colder. These strong winds could blow for days on end bringing hail, rain and even snow. We spent endless hours in our shed desperately trying to keep ourselves warm with hot-water bottles stuffed up our jerseys and drinking coffee until it came out of our ears. We also read a lot. On the whole, my taste in books seems to coincide with Annie's. I usually pack about fifty books for each season, some light and some heavy. I like to read about the area in which I am working but for light relief I turn back to Harold Robbins or Frederick Forsyth. I take music tapes along as well, mostly classical but some pop too – Abba perhaps. We both love Mastermind, jigsaws and cross-words – which is just as well as we spent a lot of time cooped up together in the shed trying to be nice to each other when all we really wanted was to be out filming.

On 30 November, we both went to bed at around nine, our usual time. It was cold and although getting into our sleeping bags was always a struggle, it was a routine we had to go through if we wanted to stay warm. Over our thermal underwear, we put on our pyjamas. Then we had to climb into the inner lining, wriggle down into our sheepskin bags and finally, somehow or other, insert the whole thing into down-filled sleeping bags. That alone was enough to tire us out and after a hard day's filming we fell asleep straight away – to be wakened an hour later by the ear-splitting noise of wind hammering against the shed.

This time it seemed more serious than the sixty-mph wind we had become used to and I poked my head up a little out of the warmth of the sleeping bag to investigate. Before going to bed, I always unzipped the flap of the tent in order to let in some fresh air. Now, peering out, I could see that something was wrong. Was it the roof of the shed or the floor? Slowly my attention focused on the walls of the shed and I realised, to my horror, that they were moving in and out as they took the full weight of the gale.

Outside, the thundering howl grew louder while inside the beams creaked and groaned and we felt the floor shifting underneath us. I thought of the other gale and the ruined wreck of the shed outside and wondered if ours was to meet the same fate. The walls shuddered under the force of each terrible impact and I held my breath, expecting to hear the sound of splintering wood. Finally, we could stand it no longer and pulling our clothes on over our pyjamas, we went outside. I lost contact with Annie straight away, each of us battling to remain on our feet. I decided to push my way round to the back of the shed where we kept our rubber boat tied up. With my face down against the battering turmoil, I clung to the side walls and began edging my way round. An extra strong blast flattened me against the shed taking my breath away and through the darkness I heard a sudden cry from Annie. She had been lifted off her feet and flung into a pile of old wire fencing. As I reached

44

the corner of the shed, I found to my dismay that the boat was gone, the frayed end of the rope flapping violently against the wall of the shed. I swung my torch round in the hope that it might not be too far away but I could see nothing. It was pointless to venture away from the shed in the height of the storm as it was impossible to stand up straight without holding on to something. Even the two aerial poles which had been supported by steel girders were now lying flat on the ground. There seemed little we could do except return to the hut to sit it out, which we did – for another three hours.

The following morning was miserable with rain clouds lying at ground level all day. We found the boat some hundred yards away, ripped and punctured on the rocks, the floorboards badly damaged. We carried it back to the shed with all the other bits and pieces we had found. It didn't take long to realise that with the few patches and glue I had I wasn't going to be able to repair it. Instead, we cleaned it up and packed it away in its box. Next we tackled the broken aerial poles and spent several hours digging deep holes in which to set the poles, this time with stronger guy ropes. We also went out to check on our two tents which we had carefully placed among the tussock grass. The first tent was fine but the second one had a badly damaged fly-sheet which we took back to the shed and repaired. When the sun finally decided to come out we grabbed our cameras and moved off. The wind, however, was still blowing at around sixty knots and we laughed at the near impossibility of trying to walk into it with all our camera equipment. Bent nearly double and forcing our way against the wind with our heavy rucksacks on our backs it looked as though we were doing some kind of dance – one step forward, two steps back. Every now and then the wind would drop without warning and both of us would hurtle forward to fall flat on our faces. Often the wind literally stopped us dead in our tracks and no matter how hard we tried, we simply could not make any headway. Annie was often spun round in circles as the tripod she was carrying was caught in a sudden gust. We filmed the rough seas, now flattened by the strong off-shore wind and we also went along to the burnt-out areas to film the impressive dust storms caused by the wind picking up the loose top soil and whirling it around. Having got what we wanted on film, we turned back for the shed and this time made it in double quick time with the wind behind us. We tore along, sometimes completely out of control, falling every now and then into the burrows of some poor unfortunate Magellan penguin.

One day, Annie and I decided to try eating tussock grass. I had been told it was very good to eat either raw or boiled and indeed it was. Now every time we went past some we would pull up a large clump, peel back all the outside leaves to get to the soft heart. It reminded us of chestnuts.

There was an area near our shed where we liked to sit at the end of the day. Round about were a lot of Magellan burrows, all of them in use. In the beginning, the penguins would do a nose-dive into their burrows whenever either of us passed by but after a few weeks they became quite used to us and as long as we went along fairly slowly and carefully, they would just stand and watch us. We spent many pleasant evenings sitting watching them. There would always be one or two penguins collecting nesting material, usually tussock grass. They would collect so much in one go that often they were unable to see properly through the grass as it flapped round their faces. They would totter back, going roughly in the direction of their burrows, tripping over little stones, falling down into burrows and sometimes getting so lost and confused that they would end up going round and round in circles. Eventually, they would stop and peer through the flapping grass to get a new bearing before pressing on again.

This Magellan area, however, could be very dangerous for us, especially after a good soaking from the rain. Although we could see the burrow entrances and easily avoid these, it was difficult to know exactly in which direction the tunnel went and often we would break through the ground sometimes falling heavily down into them. We would find ourselves flat on our faces only a few inches from a very indignant penguin making rude noises about its damaged burrow. One day, Annie went crashing through a burrow, breaking right into the nesting chamber where not only was there a penguin but also two chicks, now half buried under the soil. As Annie hit the ground, her right hand broke through into a second burrow and damaged that as well, scaring the daylights out of another penguin. I picked up the two half-buried chicks and cleaned them up by blowing gently onto their grey, fluffy down. We cleared out the nesting chamber and laid them back carefully inside. As I did so, the adult, who was still in the nest, took a hearty nip out of my hand – and penguins have very sharp little beaks. The other burrow had only suffered tunnel damage so we left it, not wanting to risk another nip. Later on in the day, on our way home from filming, we checked the two burrows and found all was well.

One calm but cloudy day, while we were returning from doing some recording, we heard a most extraordinary noise and not one that we could easily identify. When you know you are the only human beings on a deserted island even the most familiar noises sound strange. The noise we heard seemed like a fog-horn on a big boat which, of course, was unlikely. Blast after blast came to us over the hill and we decided to climb to the top of the ridge to investigate. To our utter amazement, we saw the *Forrest* cruising down the west side of the island, sounding her horn. We both waved madly and the ship turned round heading back for our shed. It was a lovely surprise as we hadn't been expecting any visitors for another four weeks. With Christmas only six days away, however, *Forrest* had called to deliver a mass of mail and quite a few Christmas gifts as well from the islanders. There were eggs, butter, cream, and Christmas pudding, among other things. We spent an hour on board *Forrest* talking to Jack Sollis and the crew, catching up on the latest news and poring over a whole bundle of old English newspapers – a great treat.

Although I had half hoped it might rain on Christmas Day – thus giving us a day off from work – I really wanted to get on with the filming as time was running out. As it happened, Christmas 1979 on Steeple Jason was not one of our best days. It poured with rain, was bitterly cold and a wind howled all day long, though only forty miles away, on another island, the sun shone most of the day. We naturally missed our families and thought about what they would be doing – struggling through huge lunches and dinners and opening presents. We consoled ourselves by talking about what we would most like to do when we got back to England. Soaking in a hot bath was at the top of the list and being able to drink fresh milk was another. Annie has a great passion for horses and a day at the races was to be one of her first treats. We both like gardening and we spent a lot of time dreaming of what I would plant in the garden of my cottage in Norfolk. Annie got carried away and started talking about new curtains, fresh wallpaper, a redesigned kitchen and just for a moment we were back in England on a summer's day, sitting in a green and sweet-smelling country garden. Reality, however, battered at the hut and we decided it was time to open our special treat which we had saved specially for Christmas – a bottle of port. We opened a couple of presents and by the time we had finished the port we were feeling quite jolly. Christmas lunch consisted of our last scrap of mutton, given to us by the crew of *Forrest* and which was now in danger of walking out of the shed. We made it into a stew with tinned carrots and instant mashed potatoes. Delicious! In the evening, we listened to the local radio and were quite touched to hear our names mentioned and to be wished a Merry Christmas by all.

Forrest was due to collect us from Steeple Jason on 10 January to take us, via Westpoint Island, back to New Island where I wanted to complete the filming of the penguins. On our last evening, when all our filming was finished, we took a cup of tea and went to sit outside in the dying sun, surrounded by Magellan penguins. There wasn't a cloud in the sky and the air was still and warm. It was easy to forget the cold and damp, the terrible November storm. Now, we simply felt sad to be leaving.

MV *Forrest* turned up next day to take us off Steeple. We had kept in radio contact all day wondering if the wind would be too strong and the Captain might change his mind about landing. However, for the fourth time running, luck was with us and the boat arrived without mishap.

It took us all the time available to pack up everything and clean out the shed. There were endless trips down to the beach, carrying cameras, film equipment, petrol generators and gas cylinders which we left on the beach ready to be loaded on board. By four p.m. everything was safely stored in the hold and we took one last sad look at Steeple Jason before steaming away.

The sea journey was rough and the Captain kindly took a slightly longer route to Westpoint Island so that we could get a little shelter from the other islands in the Jason group. The journey left us exhausted and dirty but the Napiers were so eager to hear our news that it was nearly two in the morning before we got to bed. Then we found the bedroom hot and stuffy and very quiet after Steeple Jason. We missed the din of the penguins calling to each other all night and the sheets and blankets made us toss and turn uncomfortably.

We had an early start aboard *Forrest* the next morning and were able to set out for New Island by six. It looked like being another day of green seasickness but we received an unexpected reprieve. The boat developed engine trouble and we had to turn back. Although it was only a temporary reprieve, it was nonetheless welcome. We returned to the Napiers where we spent some time going through the Christmas mail that had only just reached us. There were the two Christmas stockings which my mother had sent. I had Annie's which I had to pack up and give to her and Annie had mine. My mother had also sent us some very welcome woolly jerseys as well as hats and scarves. In all, we had two enormous post bags full of mail. Still exhausted after our sea journey, we had a quick sleep before setting out, finally this time, for New Island. Another five-hour journey steaming against the wind and tide left us feeling sick and wretched. This time, Ian and Maria Strange had got our hut warmed and cosy for our return and their eager welcoming faces told us they wanted to hear all our news. Although I was ready to collapse straight into bed, I realised that it was going to be the small hours again before I got there.

4

ROCKHOPPERS AND GENTOOS

It was two months since I had been filming on New Island. Before we'd left, Annie and I had seen the first four rockhopper penguins hop ashore on 9 October and later that afternoon, we had seen the next seven arrive. From then on, they came ashore daily in increasing numbers, popping out of the sea like corks to land on a large flat rock before starting the long journey up the cliffs to their colony.

Long, long ago when the Antarctic was warm, the penguins lost the use of their wings and became flightless. As the Antarctic grew colder, the flightless penguins were forced back into the sea to find their food and they learned to become superb under-water swimmers, propelling themselves along using their short, stubby wings. There are eighteen species of penguin with fifteen of them living north of the Antarctic Circle. The main food of all penguins is squid, small fish and krill (*Euphausia Superba*) – a shrimp-like creature. Penguins are preyed on by sea-lions and leopard seals and the great skua will take their eggs and even their chicks during the breeding season. Penguins are also very gregarious, going out to sea in large parties to catch food, and their colonies can sometimes number hundreds of thousands. They spend about half their lives at sea. For the other half, they are forced on to land to mate, nest, rear their young and moult.

The raucous cackle of the rockhoppers makes them the noisiest of all the penguins. They are about eighteen inches tall with the usual black and white colouring. They have orange beaks and pink feet but most distinctive of all are the long yellow feathers which wave above their bright red eyes. They move either by walking upright like humans or jumping from rock to rock with their feet together. They have very sharp claws on their feet which enable them to get a firm grip on the rocks as they work their way up the cliffs. Once landed, they shake the water from their bodies and preen for a while before beginning the long, tiring climb to the clifftop. The set paths to the colonies are narrow, forcing them to go in single file. Deep vertical grooves in the rocks made by the sharp claws on their feet prove that the penguins have been using the same route for years and probably for centuries.

Rockhopper colonies can be found on rocks and ledges and on steep bluffs high above the sea. One all the penguins have arrived and paired up, they settle down to breeding. They dig small depressions in the ground with their feet and then steal bits of grass and pebbles from each other to line the nests. They always seem to be fighting, biffing with their flippers and nipping with their sharp beaks. I saw one or two penguins literally covered with blood. They call all the time, even at night, and we could hear them clearly a good mile away in our hut. Almost immediately on arrival, the rockhoppers mate, the female lying down on her nest and the male climbing up onto her back, holding onto the feathers on the top of her head, digging his claws into her back and slowly moving himself into position. Both sexes look similar.

They lay two white eggs during the first week in November and the second egg is always larger than the first. I was extremely lucky, one sunny Sunday morning, to come across a female rockhopper in the process of laying an egg. At first, I wasn't sure what was going on as they usually lay their eggs at night. The female was standing up with her back to me, but every few seconds her flippers would rise up into the air and then down again to her side. She appeared to be making an awful lot of effort over something. I continued watching her and then she lay down, her back still towards me. I noticed the beginning of a white egg appearing from her rear end. My camera was out in a flash and I began filming. Every time she pushed hard, the egg would move out a little bit more and her flippers would go up in the air and down again. During all of this, the male stood quietly beside her, making threatening gestures at any other rockhopper. Harder and harder she pushed, more and more of the egg appeared and higher and higher went her flippers until finally the beautiful white egg rolled gently into the bottom of her nest. For a few minutes, the female didn't move, she just lay on the ground, no doubt thoroughly exhausted. Then she got up, bent over the egg, rolled it round a few times, lay down on it – and went to sleep.

Once rockhoppers have laid their eggs, they are very reluctant to move out of the way. It then became difficult to move amongst them. The female incubates the eggs for thirty-four days, with the male relieving her every now and then so that she can go down to the sea for a few days to feed. Once the eggs have been laid, rockhoppers have three major problems. Prolonged wet weather can cause flooding in the colony and as the penguins nest on the ground, their nests can get water-logged and half buried in the mud where the eggs grow cold and go bad. Rockhoppers who build their nests on steep-sided slopes fare much better in bad weather as the excess water can drain off. The striated caracara and the great skua are the other two problems. Should a rockhopper relax its guard over its chick or its egg even for a moment, one of the two birds will swoop down and snatch the egg or chick. I got a lot of film showing both the striated caracara and the skua taking eggs from the colony. Every day they swooped up and down, on the look-out. Sometimes, they would hover just a few feet above the penguins' heads, hoping to upset the birds enough to make them move off the nests and so expose the eggs. Every now and then, either a striated caracara or a skua would fly off with an egg in its beak, hotly pursued by several other birds. I actually saw a skua swallow a whole egg in flight because it was being chased by many other skuas and it didn't want to lose its prize.

By hatching time, we had moved on to Steeple Jason and we continued filming the rockhoppers there. The first chicks appeared on 10 December. Unfortunately for the chicks, the weather during hatching week was miserably wet and cold. The colony soon became a mud bath and some of the flat parts of the massive rockhopper colony on Steeple Jason were literally swimming in water, with eggs floating all over the place, the adults covered in mud and having to stand in water-logged nests with either eggs or chicks soaked and filthy. The heavy continuous rain finished off thousands of eggs and newly hatched chicks. When the rain ceased and the sun finally came out, the adults, chicks and eggs were caked in dried mud and looked really pathetic. Eggs buried in dried-out mud stayed there for the rest of the summer. The chicks that had died from the cold were soon picked up by predatory birds. It was a bad start to the season.

Once the chicks have hatched, the adults take it in turn to guard the chicks and keep them warm during the day while the other goes off to sea to catch krill. Every evening from about four the penguins start to return to their colony where they change over duty with the sitting bird. Almost immediately, the chicks begin squeaking and pecking gently at the adults' beaks, begging for food. This encourages the adult penguin to start regurgitating krill into the back of the throat. As they lower their heads, the chicks put *their* heads into the mouth of the adult and take

53

the food. Then the chicks, their stomachs bulging, lie down and go to sleep, the adult lying down on top of them to keep them warm and safe.

The first month of the chick's life is obviously the most dangerous. Cold, wet weather can easily kill, and preying birds are after them in earnest as now they, too, have young of their own to feed. The striated caracaras will take a young penguin chick, fly back with it to the nest, tear it up into pieces and feed it to their own chicks. The skuas also will fly back to the nest and the two parent birds tear the chick apart in a sort of tug of war, swallowing the bits of penguin chick, which they then regurgitate on the ground close to their own chicks.

By the time the chicks are four weeks old they are about nine inches high with enormous stomachs. They are really too big now to be preyed upon and so they form into crèches while the adults go out to sea for food. The crèches vary in size from six to sixty – the greater the number the safer the chick. When the adult birds return to the colony in the evening, they call out and the chicks, immediately recognising their parent's voice, come to feed. The adult bird can also recognise its own offspring calling and any chick who doesn't belong soon gets a jab. During bad weather, the young chicks huddle together in their crèches, as close as possible, trying to keep warm and dry. The ones on the outside suffer the most because the temperature there is about ten degrees lower. Their down is not yet waterproof so if they get too wet and cold they die. Although the parents are out fishing at sea during the day, there are always some adult rockhoppers keeping an eye on the young chicks. These non-breeding adults are known as nursemaids.

I noticed with amusement that when the adult birds returned to the nests, the young rockhoppers would often try to get in underneath the parent, still in search of warmth and safety. There was absolutely no way the chick could get underneath, but they almost knocked the parent over in their efforts. The adult would then have to get tough with the chick and peck it sharply.

The penguins find warm weather uncomfortable because they are well insulated against the cold and therefore find it difficult to keep cool. They try to cool themselves by lying flat on the ground, spreading their flippers out, extending their feet behind them and opening their beaks to pant, rather like dogs.

By the time we returned to New Island from Steeple Jason in January, the chicks there were well over a month old. I wanted to film, in detail, the adult rockhopper climbing back up the cliffs in the evening to feed the chicks, showing how their little claws dug into the hard rock to get a better grip and how they jumped from rock to rock. There was one particular patch of rock on one of the pathways that was always wet from a tiny stream that ran out of the cliffs and dripped on to the path. I had one hilarious afternoon filming the rockhoppers crossing these rocks, many of them skidding and slipping over backwards and careering down in a headlong, uncontrolled rush, bearing down on the unfortunate penguins who were trying to get *up* the rock. Another time when I was sitting filming on a narrow stretch of the path, I felt something on my knee. Taking my eye away from the camera for a moment, I looked down to find a rockhopper actually sitting on my knee, looking up at me. It began to wobble a bit and dug its claws in to get a better grip but fell off. Much to my amazement, however, it immediately hopped back on again a few seconds later. Unfortunately, Annie wasn't near to take some photos of this rare encounter.

It was while I was filming the rockhoppers climbing up to their colony at the top of the cliff that I had a disastrous accident. I was perched on the edge of a steep cliff and, having got some very pleasing film, was just about to finish off one of the four-hundred-foot magazines when the leg of my tripod slipped on the rocks, and camera and tripod slowly began to topple. I had removed the three lenses from the camera to clean off the sea spray which was always a headache to me. As I lunged out for one of the other legs of the tripod the sheer weight of the whole thing, about forty pounds, tore it from my grasp. Unable to do anything, I watched it go over as if it were one of my own slow-motion films. I made one last attempt to save what I could by grabbing the battery lead. It held for one brief hopeful moment – and then broke under the strain and the whole thing dropped out of sight over the cliff edge.

I closed my eyes and listened to each sickening thud as the camera crashed to the bottom of the forty-foot cliff, bouncing off successive protruding rocks on its way down – and then silence. There was nothing to do but crawl out on to the edge of the cliff and look down. There, far below, it lay. The camera had broken free of the tripod and the film magazine door had burst open, releasing four hundred feet of exposed film – a whole day's filming, now lost. As I watched, a gust of wind whisked the film into the air and wound it into knots around the various startled penguins who happened to be standing nearby. Annie came up to see what had happened. I gathered up my things and together we climbed down the cliff, retrieved the tripod and the various bits of the camera and set off, silently, for home.

Ian Strange, surprised to see us home early, came over to see what had happened. The miserable remains of the camera spoke for themselves, and for the rest of the day he very kindly helped me repair some of the damage. With a vice, we straightened the parts that had been bent and I was able to replace the broken screws. One screw stubbornly refused to stay in place and I was at my wits' end to know what to do until I remembered my emergency dental kit. The filling paste which I had been given for my teeth did an excellent job of cementing the screw in place. Slowly, we began to put the whole thing together again. I then ran a hundred-foot roll through the camera and sent it by the first available Beaver float plane to Stanley and finally on to London. The motor on the camera sounded normal but I couldn't be sure. The next three weeks were agonising as I waited to hear the news from London. I was able to use one of my other two cameras but I couldn't really relax until I knew. Eventually word came through – the film was all right!

One morning, I noticed that the barograph was dropping incredibly fast – nine millibars in three hours! It was a sure sign that a storm was about to break – and what a storm. In no time at all, the wind was churning up massive waves which pounded the shoreline. The ninety-mph wind was so strong that it was difficult to stand upright and virtually impossible to walk into. I wanted to film the penguins coming ashore from the raging seas to feed their young and we set out, taking twice as long as usual, to make the journey to the colony. When we got there I could hardly believe the little creatures could survive.

A human would have been reduced to pulp on the rocks in a matter of seconds. I filmed the little rockhoppers surfing in on the fifteen-foot waves. They were thrown up into the air, battered down upon the rocks, sucked out again and then flung back onto the rocks. Somehow they survived all this and kept bobbing up to the surface determinedly trying to reach land again. Once there, they would hop like mad over the rocks in a desperate attempt to reach higher ground before the next wave caught them. Many of them did get caught and just before the huge wave crashed down upon them they would turn and lower their heads to take the full force before being tossed up into the air and drawn out to sea to start all over again.

Filming all this was exciting, but murder on the camera and lenses. Annie and I were completely soaked by the spray which, of course, was going all over the camera as well. In between every shot I had to wipe the lenses clear. We also had to be careful where we positioned ourselves. Had we been caught unawares by a wave we wouldn't have stood a chance. In the event, it was all worth it as the footage I sent back to London turned out really well.

During the second week in February thousands of extra penguins started to come ashore. These rockhoppers were last season's chicks. Every year at this time, the one-year-old rockhoppers start to pour ashore, filling up every available space around the landing area and continuing up the pathways and round the edges of the colony. For four weeks they are forced ashore to moult. This is a miserable time for the penguins. As their old feathers start to fluff up and fall out, the new plumage slowly forms underneath. During this time, as the penguins are neither waterproof nor very well insulated, they are unable to go to sea to feed and they tend to feel the cold much more than usual. Being forced to starve during this four-week moulting period, they become pretty skinny, with their breast-bone showing clearly through their feathers. Literally thousands of young rockhoppers come ashore to moult and on strong windy days it looks almost as though it were snowing, as small white feathers fly around in the wind, littering the ground several inches deep in places.

By the middle of February, the first few rockhopper chicks of the season start moving away from their colony and begin to descend the cliffs to the landing area by the sea. They make this journey slowly, stopping often and always with a few adult rockhoppers in attendance to encourage them to keep going. In and out of the moulting rockhoppers they weave their way, avoiding getting too close to them for fear of being jabbed by those sharp beaks. Once the chicks have reached the landing area, they hang around for a few days waiting for the groups to grow in size. The chicks have now lost all their down and their smart, sleek plumage is fully waterproof and insulated. I had expected the young chicks to jump straight into the sea but they don't. They appear nervous about entering the water and walk slowly down to the edge and peer into the sea. If a small wave breaks over them they immediately turn round and hop up the rocks to safety. Only with encouragement from the adults will they return again to the water's edge.

Finally, some of the adult rockhoppers dive into the sea, usually from a small rock with a four- to six-foot drop. As soon as the chicks see the adults diving in they try to pluck up enough courage to follow suit. Some of the brave ones do take the plunge, jumping in feet first, breaking surface, paddling round for a few seconds, their heads above the water, before they dive under the water and away. More and more of the chicks jump into the sea, momentarily breaking surface, then

57

disappearing under the water. This was the last we ever saw of the chicks. From now on, they would be on their own, looking after themselves and finding their own food. The adults returning with food to their empty nests soon get the message.

At this point the rockhopper colony becomes fairly quiet. The chicks have gone and the breeding adults are no longer returning to feed their young. Instead, they go to sea for a week or so to feed up and get themselves fat. Soon they will have to return to the island to start moulting. The only rockhoppers around are the thousands of immature birds who have nearly finished their moulting. With most of their old plumage gone and their new plumage well on the way to completion, they spend a lot of time preening themselves using the oil gland at the base of their backs to waterproof their feathers.

It is not until the second week of March, when the weather has begun to deteriorate, with snow, hail and sixty-mph winds blowing all the time, that the adult rockhoppers return to the island to start their moult. The immature rockhoppers have finished moulting and are on their way back to the sea. The adult rockhoppers pour ashore in their thousands spilling over the rocks to pack tight pathways leading up to their old colonies, and for them, too, it is a bad time. They are miserable while moulting and with tempers short there are many bloody fights. First their black feathers begin to turn a dark chocolate brown in colour, then the feathers begin to fluff out and eventually fall out. A thick mass of feathers litters the ground and with all the rain and heavy spray from the sea below and with tens of thousands of little penguin feet treading the feathers into the soft ground, the whole area soon turns into a stinking mud bath, knee-deep in places.

It was really lethal for Annie and myself walking along the steep-sided cliffs over slippery rocks. Squelching through the thick, reeking mud to film the final stages of the rockhoppers' story, we slithered in the mud, often having to crawl up the slopes on our hands and knees, dragging the tripods and cameras behind us. It had got so cold that by late March we could only bear to be out on the exposed cliffs for a few hours at a time. Then we would go back to the hut and gulp some hot coffee and thaw out a little before returning to the cliffs. Up on the cliffs in the full force of a fifty-mph wind, the temperature plummeted to an alarming degree. Annie, in fact, got something called frost-burn in her left foot — the beginning of frost-bite. While filming, we had to position ourselves with our backs to the wind, otherwise we found our faces, if they caught the wind broadside on, turning numb in the cold.

Often while up on the cliffs watching the rockhoppers, we would get caught in a blizzard or a fierce hail storm and we had to find what shelter we could in the tussock grass.

By mid-April, I had completed the rockhopper film. The adult penguins had finished moulting and had produced immaculate new plumage. As soon as they were ready, they headed for the sea and dived in, eager to start hunting for food. With each passing day, more and more penguins left the colony to go fishing though always returning for the night. After about four days, the number of penguins returning in the evenings began to drop as more and more left for good.

By 20 April, the colony was completely deserted. Nothing moved. No sound could be heard except for the howling wind. All the penguins had left. They had done their work and would not return for six months. Wandering around the deserted colony, we saw the remains of a few well-grown chicks who had not made it to the sea and these were being picked up by the ever-present striated caracaras and skuas. Soon, these too would disappear.

Although our film had been mainly about the rockhoppers, we also spent a good deal of time, especially on New Island, observing and filming another member of the penguin family – the gentoos.

These penguins are bigger and heavier than the rockhoppers with a red bill and a distinguishing white triangular flash across the forehead from eye to eye. Their average weight is about twelve pounds.

Gentoo colonies, always on level or gently sloping ground, vary from several pairs to hundreds. No matter what the colony's size or the space available, the pairs build their nests close together with just enough space in between to prevent the sitting birds from reaching over and pecking each other. This can be a problem for the birds whose nests are deep in the colony as they have to run the gauntlet through the narrow passages between each nest, often receiving sharp jabs in the body from the sitting birds defending their small nesting area.

Their nests are small depressions in the ground built up around the edges with grass and small stones. The male collects most of the nesting material while the female sits in her nest arranging the material around her. The nests round the edge of the colony are relatively easy to build, as the male has to wander off only a short distance, to find all the material he wants. The ones in the middle have a bigger problem. The male is open to repeated attacks as he journeys to and fro collecting his nesting material but he may choose a very much easier, quicker and safer method – pinching material from nearby nests. He will watch his neighbours carefully until they are looking in the opposite direction or have dropped off to sleep for a few minutes, then quickly picking up a beakful of their nesting material, he will proudly present it to his mate. They have great patience and we watched one bird replace a stone eleven times before it remained in position.

Gentoos lay two white eggs in late October which both sexes incubate until they hatch, forty to forty-one days later. When the pair change places at the nest, the relieved partner, in no particular hurry, stays close by the nest, stretching and preening and sometimes going off to collect more nesting material. Eventually, the bird will set off for the sea where it may spend several days feeding and building up fat reserves.

In early December, the two down-covered chicks hatch within twenty-four hours of one another. For the first six weeks of their lives, they stay in the nest protected by the parents who keep them warm and well fed on krill, small fish and squid. After about six weeks, the chicks start to form up into crèches while their parents leave the colony to go fishing. They spend most of the day sleeping flat out, their flippers extended and their feet protruding at the back with the undersides up. It is not until the early afternoon that they begin to wake up and become more active. They play around, chasing each other, examining sticks, broken eggshells or anything else that might catch their fancy – picking them up and running around with them. Flapping their flippers, they jump up and down, sometimes careering around in circles. As the afternoon progresses, they start to watch out for their parents returning from the sea with food, for by now the chicks are very hungry.

The adults call out as they arrive back at the colony and when the chicks reach the adult they beg for food by nibbling at the parent's beak. After a short time, the parent regurgitates the food which it has stored in its stomach. However, things don't always proceed as smoothly as that. Often, other chicks will come bounding up to the feeding adults and disturb them, causing the parent bird to stop feeding its own chicks. The strategy then, for the parent bird, is to run through the colony with its own chicks – plus the visitor – in hot pursuit, tripping over empty nests and bumping into other birds until, eventually, the unwanted chick gives up the chase. Then the adult will stop and start to feed its own chicks once again. The aim of this chase is two-fold. Not only does it provide the young birds with some much-needed exercise but it also trains them to go in search of food for themselves. Sometimes, although the adults have finished feeding their young, the chicks will continue to beg for food. The parent bird will peck and lash out with its flipper to discourage the begging but often the chick pays no attention and will continue until the adult is forced, yet again, to set off through the colony followed by the chicks who, this time hampered by full stomachs, give up the chase.

When the chicks are about three months old and feeding has become less and less, they venture away from their colony down to the sandy beaches, playing amongst the seaweed and going out to the surf until they dive into the sea and away they go, totally independent.

The adults stay at sea for a few weeks, fattening themselves up before coming ashore again for their moult. For many days, we watched the gentoos arriving up the sandy beach, on their way to their colony. Occasionally alone, but usually in large groups of fifty or more, they would first appear far out at sea porpoising towards the shore. Once they were within a short distance of the beach, they would dive under water and with powerful strokes from their flippers, gather up enough momentum to explode out of the surf, sailing a good foot clear of the water, to land on the beach either on their feet or on their stomach, occasionally tumbling or somersaulting as well. They would sort themselves out and hurry up the beach where they would join the other penguins resting and preening themselves after their landing.

For two weeks, we concentrated our filming on the sandy beaches where the gentoos had landed, in order to film their main predator – the sea-lion. There are various telltale signs to give warning that a sea-lion is about. Giant petrels in small groups sitting on the water near the beach is a sure sign. Another is a group of gentoos behaving in a rather nervous and hesitant way on the beach, obviously wanting to enter the water to go fishing but reluctant to do so. The sea-lion will wait on the edge of a kelp bed. This kelp – a type of seaweed – forms a perfect hiding place from which the sea-lion can suddenly launch a surprise attack upon a party of gentoos returning from the sea. Or perhaps the sea-lion will swim lazily up and down the bay every now and then breaking surface to breathe and try to catch an isolated gentoo moving slowly through the water with a full stomach after a day's fishing.

Once the sea-lion has picked its victim, the chase begins. It is a very exciting chase with the odds slightly against the penguin getting away. Its tactic is to zigzag furiously and sharply so that the sea-lion, which can swim faster but cannot turn as quickly, soon gives up the chase, swimming off lazily in the other direction where it will have a rest before picking out another victim. The gentoo which has just escaped will swim swiftly for the beach, popping out of the surf and running up the beach until it is out of harm's way, still panting heavily. Some penguins, of course, don't make it. Often the sea-lion will catch up with a penguin and pull it down under water, coming up repeatedly to thrash it on the surface and usually tearing off a flipper or a leg or opening up its stomach. Once the penguin is fatally wounded or dead, the sea-lion swims slowly round it, nudging it every now and then, sometimes taking a bite out of it. More often than not, however, the sea-lion loses interest in its victim once it is dead. It may play around with the body for a short while, throwing it up into the air or continuing to thrash it around but it soon gets bored with the lack of response and goes off to find another bird to chase.

After the kill, the giant petrels enter the scene. As soon as the sea-lion moves off, leaving a bloody and torn penguin floating on the water, the birds move in and eat whatever is left. The oil from one penguin can stretch out for several hundred feet, making it obvious why, not so long ago, these little creatures were ruthlessly clubbed to death, some even being thrown live into boiling tripots, for their oil.

I wanted to record in super-slow motion, the sea-lion chasing the penguin, as well as the gentoos landing on the beach. The camera I was using, which had been lent to me by Survival in London, was large and heavy and so was the big twenty-seven-volt battery which powers it. When turned to full speed, the camera would run at two hundred frames per second, roughly five feet of film per second and it was terribly important that I loaded and laced the film exactly right so that it ran smoothly through the gate of the camera. Every day for two weeks or more, we would walk down to the south end of New Island where the gentoos had their colony and where they landed on the beautiful white shining beach. Many days, we would set out laden with equipment, the sun shining in a clear blue sky, but after a few minutes on the beach and just when we had set up the cameras, the clouds would appear and it would start to rain. Once it even started snowing. Then we would have to pack up all the cameras again and struggle the two miles back to our hut. Other days, however, the sunny weather would hold and we would spend the afternoon sitting on the beach waiting for the action.

When the sea-lion actually breaks surface and thrashes the gentoo on the top of the water, it lasts in normal motion, perhaps one second. It is all over so quickly that, when you first see it, you wonder just what it was you saw. So once the chase was on, I had to follow with my camera, focusing the whole time. Annie's job was to switch on the camera just as the sea-lion came to the top. It required split-second coordination between the two of us and though we exhausted ourselves running up

Recording the
rockhoppers on
New Island

ABOVE Every evening the gentoo penguins would walk over the hill from the sea to feed their hungry chicks

LEFT A pair of gentoos mating

OPPOSITE PAGE

ABOVE LEFT A week-old gentoo chick

ABOVE RIGHT Two large gentoo chicks being fed

BELOW The sandy beach at the south end of New Island where the gentoos leave for the sea and return from feeding

A gentoo carrying a large stone back to its nest

OPPOSITE ABOVE   An aerial view of Carcass Island

OPPOSITE BELOW   The settlement on Carcass Island. The cottage where we lived is the second building on the right

A pair of red-backed buzzards. The female in the rear has the red back

OPPOSITE PAGE
ABOVE   Talking to Rob and Lorraine McGill, owners of Carcass Island, and their children Janie *(left)* and Roy *(right)*
BELOW LEFT   Feeding Senior, our tame black-crowned night heron
BELOW RIGHT   Helping to shear the sheep

ABOVE A Falkland thrush, its beak full of nesting material. It makes its nest in the gorse bushes

LEFT A black-crowned night heron with a small fish

OPPOSITE A crested caracara, locally known as a Carancho, landing on a rock

FOLLOWING PAGES The very impressive South American tern colony in full flight on Carcass Island

ABOVE A pair of
dolphin gulls mating

RIGHT A common
snipe

OPPOSITE ABOVE
Annie and me in our
flying suits with
Lt-Commander Tony
Ellerbeck, RN, from
HMS *Endurance*

OPPOSITE BELOW
With the Blue Lady,
our luxurious
transport on Carcass
Island

ABOVE A Patagonian crested duck preening on the shoreline

LEFT About to enter my underground hide to film the Magellan penguins

ABOVE A pair of Magellan penguins going through part of their courtship display

LEFT A Magellan penguin calling outside its burrow in the evening

A pair of kelp geese.
The female is the
front one

An adult king shag
on its nest

and down the beach to get ourselves in the right position at the right time, it worked very well and I got some very satisfactory slow-motion shots.

Filming gentoos landing, in slow motion, was very much easier. I could pre-focus the camera on a particular area of the beach, lock it into position and then sit beside the camera with the control switch in my hand. Annie would patrol along the beach waiting for a party of gentoos to come ashore. When the gentoos got close to the beach, however, and noticed Annie, they would veer away to land somewhere else. Annie had to keep pace with the porpoising gentoos now swimming parallel to the beach until she judged that they were more or less in the position where I wanted them to land. She would then quickly withdraw and the gentoos would turn towards the beach and, we hoped, land near the camera. As long as I stayed still and quiet, they never noticed me with the camera. Most of the time it worked well and I got some good shots. I remember one afternoon, though, when the gentoos took no notice of Annie who was jumping up and down on the beach yelling at the penguins to go back and land somewhere else. The gentoos landed exactly where she was standing, pouring ashore all round her, some dashing in between her legs and then, after hurrying up the beach, stopping to look back at her in a startled and confused way. I just sat and laughed until my jaws ached.

We spent many beautiful sunny evenings at the gentoos' colony filming the chicks waiting in their crèches for their parents to return to feed them. A lot of the chicks were moulting their fluffy down and their new plumage was starting to appear. At this stage in their lives, the young gentoos are very inquisitive and, seeing us sitting quietly with our cameras, would creep up on us, a few steps at a time. When they had got to within a few feet of us, they would stand and stare and, moving their heads from side to side, would gently nibble at the legs of the tripod or even peer down the lens of my camera. Sometimes we would find one with its head poking into our rucksack to find out what was inside.

Eventually the adult gentoos would appear over the hill and waddle down to the colony in single file. As soon as the chicks saw their parents they would forget all about us and rush off. The sight of the adults coming down the hill in a long line, white against the green hillside, on a calm summer evening is one I shall never forget.

5

THE CALL OF
THE FALKLANDS

With the first season's filming completed, Annie and I returned to England in May 1980. Back home, we had the mammoth task of sorting through all the material we had collected. More research had to be done and an accompanying script written before the film, which we called *Penguin Island*, could be shown by Survival.

By September, however, we were both ready – and eager – to return to the South Atlantic, this time to Carcass Island where I hoped to make my next film about the Magellan penguins and also get some film of the ducks and geese which inhabit Carcass. Our departure from England this time was a lot easier. MV *Forrest* had already transported all our equipment from New Island to Carcass and I had made arrangements with Rob McGill, the owner of the island, to use one of the two cottages in the main settlement. On 24 September 1980, Annie and I arrived on Carcass – our home for the next seven months.

Carcass Island which is in the West Falklands is about four thousand acres in size. It is named after HMS *Carcass*, the naval vessel which anchored in the harbour in 1765 to take some soundings. Much later, in 1872, the island was leased as a sealing base to Charles Hansen, a Dane. He began to stock it with sheep and cattle and his son, Jason, later bought the freehold of Carcass as well as that of the Jason Islands. The son concentrated on developing the sheep which he imported from New Zealand. In winter, the short island grass is covered in snow and the sheep have nowhere to graze. Jason Hansen soon realised the value of the tussock grass as a winter fodder and set about fencing it off. With only two men to help him, he also took on the long and back-breaking task of planting new tussock grass to replace that which had been over-grazed. By 1940, the job had been completed and all the sheep on Carcass were wintered in the tussock paddocks.

The island had changed hands a few times since then, but the present owners, Rob and Lorraine McGill have devoted themselves to its conservation, fencing off part of the island and leaving it for the wildlife to breed there undisturbed.

Rob and Lorraine are both Falkland Islanders and though Rob, in his earlier days, has been abroad, Lorraine has never left the islands and says that she has no wish to – she is quite happy living on Carcass with Rob and their two children, Roy and Janie.

Valley Cottage, which they agreed to rent to us, is the oldest cottage on the island. When we arrived, we found it had been freshly painted and had new plumbing and wiring installed, making it warm, cosy and very comfortable. The main house, where the McGills lived was down by the harbour, a few yards from the shore. Our cottage was four hundred yards further up a gentle slope which gave us a marvellous view of the whole south-east end of the island and the harbour. There was a fine old paraffin Aga cooker in the sitting-room which kept the room warm and provided us with hot water. It was a great luxury to return in the evenings to a warm room and to be able to have a hot bath as well. The McGills kept us well supplied with milk, eggs, butter and fresh mutton – and anything else we needed.

A small flower garden grew around the cottage, well protected from the strong winds by a thick boxwood hedge. We took great delight in our gardening. We even had a vegetable patch round the back which the McGills had planted with potatoes, carrots, cabbages, cauliflowers and lettuces. Once planted, it was up to us to make them grow, which we did very successfully.

With Valley Cottage, we inherited a tame black-crowned night heron mysteriously called Senior. Morning and evening, Senior would arrive on our doorstep waiting to be fed with either raw mutton or fish that we had caught in the harbour. So long as we opened the door slowly and sat down gently by him, he wouldn't move away. We would then offer him fairly large chunks of meat and fish which he would take from our hands. If he was very hungry, he also had a go at our fingers which could be more than a little painful. Senior would continue feeding until, with his gullet bulging out at the side of his neck, it was impossible to fit any more food in. He would then hop up into one of the boxwood hedges and sit there for a little while before flying off. If Senior got bored waiting for us – he expected the door to open the moment he arrived – he would either fly up onto the tin roof and charge about up there making the most infernal noise or he would perch on the boxwood hedge just outside the window and peer in growling until one of us got up to feed him. He was quite a character.

After our arrival, Rob brought out a 1954 Land Rover which had been lying in the peat shed and with a lot of tinkering managed to get it going. We ripped off the very tatty canvas cover and replaced it with a slightly better one which we found in the shed. A couple of times the Blue Lady, as we called her, stopped dead – always at the furthest possible point from the settlement, which meant a long walk back for help. Once she got used to being out again all over the hills, however, she settled down and ran happily on three cylinders and occasionally four, producing a hearty backfire every now and then.

There was plenty of wildlife to film on Carcass. There are no black-browed albatross or rockhopper penguins but these I had already filmed anyway during the previous season. Instead there were huge numbers of shoreline birds with large colonies of gulls, terns, oyster catchers, geese, duck, rock and king shags, also elephant seals. There is some good tussock grass along the west side of the island which offers shelter to a mass of birds including Magellan penguins, wrens, finches, thrushes, the long-tailed meadow lark and the cheeky little tussock bird.

Running all the way down the middle of the island is a high rocky ridge standing about seven hundred feet, and up on this ridge live the birds of prey – the red-backed hawk, crested caracara, peregrine falcon, turkey vulture and the striated caracara.

The first month on Carcass was rather slow as far as filming was concerned. The weather was bitterly cold and unsettled, with strong winds, snow and hail most of the time. It was still too early in the season for most of the birds but the reason I had come to Carcass in September was to try to get some film of the elephant seal whose breeding season begins then. The summer before, hundreds of them had turned up on the sandy beaches on the north-west of the island and they had bred there fairly successfully. This year, however, only sixty had arrived. Rob's theory was that the seals were preyed upon by sea-lions and this was causing the seal population to decrease rapidly. He maintained that the sea-lions came ashore just when the female seals had started pupping and that they went round systematically maiming and killing the pups. I did, in fact, manage to film a sea-lion wandering among a small group of elephant seals which included several pups. Neither the bull, which was mating at the time, nor any of the females made any attempt to chase off the intruder. The sea-lion went right up to the pups and had a good sniff but, losing interest, turned away and went back down to the beach. It is true that the sea-lions *do* take the young pups, leaving their horribly mutilated bodies on the beach but I also think that the elephant seals are leaving Carcass Island in search of uninhabited islands, of which there are many in the Falklands group, where they can breed totally undisturbed.

I did some filming of the elephant seals but it wasn't all that successful. Little did I know that during my next season on South Georgia there would be more elephant seals than I could hope to deal with.

We had many good times with the McGills during our stay on Carcass. Once, during the November to January shearing season, Rob tried to teach me how to shear a sheep and I thought it might be fun to learn. Rob was kind and patient, stopping his work to help whenever I got into such a mess that I ended up on the floor having a wrestling match with the unfortunate animal. The first day was back-breaking. I was permanently doubled up at the waist, never able to hold the heavy mechanical shears in my hand for more than five minutes. Sweat poured off me, running down into my eyes and dripping off the end of my nose. Rob repeatedly showed me the various positions. I should hold the sheep in so that it remained still long enough to be sheared. No matter how hard I tried, however, I always wound up spread-eagled over the animal desperately trying to stop it wriggling and kicking out with its very sharp hooves. I went to bed exhausted and remained doubled up all night, unable to straighten out my aching back.

The next day, I actually managed to get one of the sheep into a comfortable position – all I had to do now was shear it! I was worried that I was going to cut the sheep with the razor-sharp shears and cause its premature death. Rob showed me how to lay the shears flat and to pull the skin of the sheep tight over the body so that there were no wrinkles for the shears to catch. The blades would then glide smoothly over the animal, cutting the wool close without cutting the skin. The sheep is placed in a different position according to which part of the animal has to be sheared – legs, back, sides, neck, head or belly. This is supposed to make it comfortable for both you and the sheep. My back, for the second day, disagreed with all this.

On the third day, I really began to enjoy myself. My back didn't ache any more and my hand didn't tire so quickly. The sheep stopped wriggling and kicking and I began to shear one sheep every five minutes. I was absolutely thrilled and now considered myself capable of shearing sheep – so I stopped, and went back to filming.

Later on in the season, when the eighteen hundred sheep had been sheared Annie and I helped with the baling. While Rob and I worked on the baling press, Annie and the children would pass up the neatly rolled fleeces. I worked the top half of the press with Rob at the bottom. Into each half we would squeeze and stamp down sixteen to twenty fleeces. The top half of the press was then lifted up by a pulley and placed over the bottom half. Finally, with poles and a ratchet, the wool was pressed through from the top half into the bottom half which had been lined with a baling sack. While Annie and I sewed up the baling sack, Rob would bind it with wire. The press was then released, the sack marked with Rob's initials and its number and weight noted. We all had a great deal of fun and laughter in the shearing shed. I'd thought Annie had managed to cut down on the number of accidents since we'd first arrived in the Falklands but I was reckoning without the carving knife. Rob McGill kept us supplied with a side of meat every ten days or so and while cutting up one of these, Annie severed a tendon with the knife. We fixed it up in a steel splint which she later wielded to great effect in a rugby match. Back at Stanley for a few days, we joined the Stanley Girls to play a match against the Royal Marines, all dressed as women. Annie and I played wings and scored seven tries and, in addition, Annie managed to blood one of the unfortunate Marines with her steel splint!

Our second Christmas in the Falklands wasn't as solitary as our first. *Then* there been only Annie and myself on Steeple Jason. This time, we had the company of four other people – Rob, Lorraine and the two children – quite a crowd! Christmas 1980 was wet, very wet, which meant we couldn't film. It was one of those days which made me think, just a little longingly, of the family gathering around a log fire. Over at the McGills', however, the Christmas spirit was flowing. The children had put up decorations and Lorraine, always a great cook, had roasted a lamb. In the afternoon, we all returned to bed, gathering strength to carry on drinking in the evening. Altogether a satisfying Christmas, although had I known what disaster was about to strike, I wouldn't have enjoyed myself quite so much.

I normally get through about forty thousand feet of film during each season. A few weeks before Christmas, I realised I was running low and asked Survival in London to send me another ten thousand feet, which they air-freighted out almost by return. Three weeks later it still hadn't arrived and I began to worry – where was it? I telexed London and they said they thought it might be in Buenos Aires. Stanley said no, *they* thought it might be in Rio de Janeiro. I asked them all to try again – harder. I now had only five hundred feet of film left and, in desperation, I called up the British Embassy in Buenos Aires to ask for their help. A few more frustrating days passed and then came word from Survival. They thought the film was still somewhere in Buenos Aires. This time, Stanley agreed and the British Embassy confirmed they had located the parcel in a warehouse at Buenos Aires International Airport, where it was stuck in a backlog of deliveries. I now had *no* film left and the only thing to do seemed to be to fly to Stanley where I could telex direct to the clearing agents in Buenos Aires, asking them to send it on the next available flight. This they tried to do, but the backlog proved bigger than the agents and they were told my film would have to wait its turn. I pleaded and begged with officials on the phone and by telex but they wouldn't budge. I asked Survival to start all over again and send some more film. My last agonising phone call was to the Managing Director of Aero Lineas Cargo Department. With the aid of an interpreter, I told my story for the hundredth time, imploring him to release the film and send it on to me. If this failed, it would have to be the President! The next day, as usual, I went to Stanley Airport, to wait forlornly for the plane from Buenos Aires. Unbelievably, my film was on it.

It was now vital to get back to Carcass as quickly as possible to make up for the lost time. That night, however, a gale blew up which lasted five days, grounding all planes. I stomped around Stanley in a terrible mood, itching to get at the cameras. It had been two weeks since I had done any filming. When I had left Carcass Island, most of the eggs had hatched. The young grow at an alarming rate and I was worried that by the time I got back the change would be noticeable in the film.

The storm finally abated and I got away to Carcass. I toured the island checking all the colonies and nests that I had been filming and found, to my relief, that only the terns had changed dramatically in my two weeks' absence. When I left, they had just hatched and now they were almost ready to fly, but there was nothing I could do about *that*.

In February, my father and youngest sister, Vicky, came out to the Falklands and stayed at Valley Cottage with us for ten days. What a wonderful time we had. The most amazing thing was that we had seven days of cloudless, warm and sunny weather which is very unusual for the Falklands. My father told me that he had never stayed with anyone before for as long as ten days, so I felt greatly honoured. Both Papa and Vicky looked drawn and pale when they arrived, but after a week of fresh air and sun and many hours spent walking all over the island, they looked as healthy as any human being can. For the first time in my life, I saw my father relaxed, really relaxed. Normally, when he says he is going to have a quiet read it means he is going to work through an enormous pile of papers or, perhaps, prepare a speech. If he *does* read, it is because he is trying to find out about something. At Valley Cottage, however, he actually sat down and read three novels – and loved every minute of it.

Papa was invaluable to me, carefully going through my filming notes and coming up with a few ideas of certain shots for sequences which were still needed for the story. It was a sad day when their visit came to an end. I flew back to Stanley with Vicky and Papa and we spent a couple of days with the Hunts in Government House. On 18 February, I flew back to Carcass and Papa and Vicky flew back to London.

We spent a great deal of our time on Carcass filming the Magellan penguin. This bird is smaller than the gentoo although slightly larger than the rockhopper. It is easily recognisable by the black and white bands which cross the throat and neck and extend down to the sides. Like the gentoo, the Magellan walks upright, but its flippers are kept either at its side or slightly forward. They are more agile among the rocks than gentoos, but less so than rockhoppers. When frightened, they toboggan rapidly over the ground, running on the tips of their toes and flippers, with their bellies held clear of the ground. Another distinctive action of the Magellan is that of cocking the head and turning it from side to side when it sees something immediately in front. It is as though the penguin cannot believe what it sees with one eye so checks with the other.

In late September, the first few Magellan penguins start to come ashore to begin their breeding season. They nest in burrows either under tussock clumps or in the hillsides. Once pairing has been accomplished, they either dig themselves into a new burrow for the season or, more usual, re-occupy a burrow from the previous season. In the southern hemisphere, September is the end of winter and the ground is therefore wet and soft. The penguins have no problem in cleaning out the burrow and lining it with fresh grass and diddle-dee which is a heather-like plant. Little clouds of earth fly out from the entrance to the burrow as one penguin works while the other rests nearby. The tunnel always slopes downwards but the floor of the nest chamber is slightly higher than the adjacent tunnel floor so that any water which runs into the burrow will collect away from the eggs. Having made their burrow dry and snug, the Magellan then go through their courtship and mating and the female returns to the burrow to lay her two white eggs in late October.

When a Magellan arrives outside its burrow, it always gives a long distinctive call and, in fact, the Magellan is locally known as the Jack-ass because of the braying sound it makes. The chest starts to heave as though it were about to be sick then, lifting its head high and opening its beak, it lets forth a series of woeful calls, each accompanied by the swelling and collapsing of the chest as it sucks air in and blows it out again. The calls slowly decrease in volume until they peter out to a few little hiccups. You can hear the Magellans calling throughout the night and rather like the cry of the fish eagle in Africa, which is often known as the 'Call of Africa', the Magellan's cry is, to me, the Call of the Falklands.

The Magellan incubates the two eggs for thirty-seven days, constantly rolling them. Both male and female incubate, changing over duty every few days. Although both sexes look alike, the male is slightly heavier in build. Every time one of the penguins arrives at the entrance to the burrow, it utters its call to its mate inside. The mate then comes out, head first, and they both then call to each other. After a few minutes, the incubating penguin wanders off through the tussock grass down to the sea to feed and the other bird disappears into the burrow to continue incubating. Every now and then, the incubating penguin, leaving the burrow to relieve itself, will do some preening and then perhaps gather some fresh grass to line the nest. It goes to nearby tussock clumps and, grabbing a small beakful, will pull and twist at the grass until it breaks away. The bird then takes the fresh grass back down inside the burrow and adds it to the nest lining.

By early December, the two eggs have hatched, with about twenty-four hours between each hatching. A tiny little bundle of grey fluffy down emerges out of the egg. Although their eyes are closed, the chicks immediately start squeaking as they make their way to the head of the adult to beg for food. The sitting bird obliges by regurgitating krill and squid into its mouth which the tiny chicks feed out of. Now the adults change over duty every day, usually in the late evening, although I also saw them change over in the morning when the chicks were a bit older. After the exchange of calls, the returning bird goes down into the burrow and the chicks immediately begin begging for food. The adult, with a ravenous chick on either side, regurgitates and turning its head feeds one after the other. The chicks, with stomachs now bulging, collapse into the deepest part of the nest and go to sleep. After a few hours, they wake up again and beg for more food and the adult again obliges until it has no more food to offer. As the chicks grow larger and their demand for food is greater, the feeding adult can only manage one feed, having to regurgitate all the food it has in one go.

The chicks grew very quickly and, with the aid of a hide, I was able to watch their progress deep down in the nest. For some time, I had been searching round for a suitable Magellan burrow. I wanted one that didn't go too far underground as this would have meant a lot of digging. I eventually found one that was only two or three feet deep under a tussock clump where the ground was fairly soft and would be easy to dig. I watched the entrance for a few days to make sure it was occupied and also to find out what stage the penguins were at. I decided not to open up the burrow until I knew the female had laid her eggs. The birds wouldn't be amused at the disturbance I was likely to cause when setting up the hide and if I waited until the eggs were laid I knew the parents would be much less likely to desert. Every evening I would visit the burrow and, kneeling down at the entrance, shine a torch down the tunnel until I could see the bird. Then, with the help of a long bamboo stick, I would gently ease the female up to see if she had laid her eggs. When I saw the first of her two eggs, I gave her another twenty-four hours to lay the second and then began to build the hide.

The last time I had built a hide had been in very different conditions. I had been in Africa making a film about kingfishers and had wanted to film the parents feeding their young. My source of light then had been the sun, aided and abetted by a piece of tin-foil! This, however, was my first effort at building a hide for Magellans.

I cut away half of the tussock clump that grew over the burrow and dug into the hillside until I knew that I was well below the level of the nest. Then, very carefully, I started to pull away more of the tussock grass at the level of the nest until, finally, I broke through into the chamber. The sitting penguin did not take kindly to having its home half-demolished and started to stab viciously at my hand with its beak. Not wanting to upset the bird more than I had to, I covered up the small hole I had made with a wooden board and withdrew for a while to allow the bird to settle down again. After an hour, I returned and continued to increase the size of the hole until I had exposed the whole nesting chamber. I was amazed that the sitting penguin remained in the burrow the whole time although it did peck my hands several times – hard enough to draw blood. Having exposed the nest, I replaced the board and left.

For the next two days, I built a wooden hide just big enough for myself, a small camera and my lights. One side of the hide had no wall and this was the end I put up tight against the tussock clump. I threw a tarpaulin over the whole thing to make it waterproof and installed my small cold-lights with the twelve-volt battery they run off – and a wooden box to sit on.

The first time I sat in the hide, I kept the lights off. At this stage, I simply wanted the penguins to get used to me. Carefully taking away the wooden board, I found there was just enough light coming down the tunnel for me to make out the bird on the nest. For three hours, I sat hunched up, hardly moving a muscle, watching the penguin. Every now and then, it would pick up a bit of nesting material and rearrange it, or maybe rise a little off the eggs to roll them with its beak. At one point, I watched its eyes slowly begin to close as it had a little sleep – a very good sign.

I spent two more sessions without lights and when I did switch them on, I used very low wattage bulbs that produce only a faint glow rather like a solitary candle. For the next few sessions, I used this bulb until I was sure the penguins were quite relaxed and then I gradually increased the light until I had enough to film. All this took about ten days.

The first time they heard the camera, the penguins jumped but as it wasn't a very loud noise, they soon got used to it. I spent countless enjoyable hours first with the two Magellan penguins and later with their chicks, watching and recording on film their secret lives inside the burrow.

The cold-lights I was using produce light but no heat and they are especially suitable for use in confined places where the bulbs and the small subjects might otherwise become over-heated. Another method is to use ordinary film lights and train a fan on the subject. The important thing was to ensure the chicks did not become over-heated and uncomfortable. For me, it was another story altogether as life inside the hide was far from pleasant at times. After a long session, lasting sometimes up to twelve hours without a break, I would end up with stiff legs and an appalling backache. A flask of hot coffee and sandwiches kept me going and while the penguins were asleep I was sometimes able to read although, when not filming, I would use a very low wattage bulb to conserve the energy in the battery.

When the eggs had hatched and the two chicks were a week old the smell in the burrow became almost unbearable. The two chicks would defecate inside the burrow, turning the tussock grass lining into a sodden, stinking mass. Flies came down the tunnel and laid their eggs in this filthy mess to produce thousands of tiny white grubs. These crawled all over the burrow and, to my horror, invaded the hide as well. One particular day, the smell was so suffocating that I had to abandon the burrow for some fresh air to clear my head. Another problem was the number of tiny fleas that inhabit the plumage of the Magellan penguin. Too small to see, I certainly felt them as they crawled up my trouser leg and inside my shirt and I would scratch until I was raw. It was an unwritten law that, for several hours after I had come out of the hide, I should stay away from Lorraine as she was very sensitive to flea bites.

With the parents now changing over duty every twenty-four hours and constantly providing food for them, the chicks developed rapidly. After three weeks, when they were about nine inches high and covered in a pale grey down, they began to venture up the tunnel. Every day they would creep a little further up on their bellies, with the sitting adult remaining behind in the nest chamber. When the chicks were about four weeks old, I could just make out their heads slightly below the level of the burrow entrance. On warm days the adult would lie outside sleeping in the sun and occasionally preening the chicks' heads.

By now it was early January and the adults and the chicks were spending most of their time outside the burrow. Both Annie and I would spend all day, only ten feet away, filming the small family gathering. The penguins paid little attention to us, only looking up and watching us should we move suddenly or cough or sneeze. Feeding took place outside the burrow and, in fact, the only time they went back inside was when the weather turned nasty.

By the end of January, the two chicks started to moult their baby down. Their flippers were the first to go, then their fronts and backs, starting at the base and gradually working up until the down remained only on the neck and head. The chicks were now fully out in the open and spending a lot of time preening and oiling their new feathers.

One lovely sunny afternoon in early February, the eldest chick wandered away from the burrow, down the gently sloping tussock hill towards the sea. The adults had changed over duty and one was now ready to return to the sea. It set off with the chick following, but progress was slow as the chick, unable to keep up, would stop and look back in the direction of the burrow as if a little reluctant to leave the safety and warmth of its home. Gradually, however the journey down the hill was made and a couple of days later, the second chick set off.

When they arrived at the sea, they joined up with groups of other Magellans along the shore. These penguins consisted of non-breeding adults and immatures who had started to come ashore to moult. The two chicks spent a short while preening and oiling their feathers. Then, when they were quite ready, they entered the sea and vanished. The two adults, having successfully completed the rearing of their chicks, went to sea for a week or so to fatten up before their own moult.

By mid-April, the tussock grass and hillsides were quiet and still. All the Magellans had left and for the next five months they would live at sea, feeding and resting until the next season drew them back to the islands. It was time for us to leave Carcass Island, too. We had loved every minute of our stay, especially the luxury of Valley Cottage. It was always tempting to return to the warm sitting-room when we were filming out in the cold. Instead of having to walk everywhere, we had the Blue Lady to transport both us and our equipment, and with a hot bath and a real loo to sit on, what more could we have asked for? The kindness of Rob and Lorraine was quite amazing, especially as it never diminished once during the seven months of our stay.

In late April the Royal Navy's ice-patrol ship, *Endurance*, turned up to collect us from Carcass. Because it was a naval vessel, special permission had to be sought from the Ministry of Defence before we could be allowed to sleep on board. Pick-up day was very foggy and we seriously wondered if we would get off the island. However, we were picked up without mishap and taken on board *Endurance* to meet the Captain, Nick Barker, who was to become a very good friend.

On board *Endurance*, we began the first leg of our journey home. Ahead of us lay a full summer of work, putting together the next Survival film, which was to be called *Falkland Summer*. As well as working on the film, however, my other major task was to try to persuade the British Antarctic Survey, known as BAS, to allow us to set up camp on South Georgia, an island which lies about eight hundred miles south-east of the Falklands. BAS has a permanent base there and I hoped that with the cooperation of the BAS team I would be able to make my third and final film on the wildlife of the South Atlantic.

6

GATEWAY TO
THE ANTARCTIC

My attempts to persuade the British Antarctic Survey to allow me to spend some months filming on South Georgia finally proved successful – though it had taken a lot of hard talking.

British scientists have been making studies in the Antarctic since 1925. In 1959, Britain became one of twelve nations to sign the Antarctic Treaty the aim of which was to maintain the continuation of scientific research and to ensure that the continent would be used for peaceful purposes only. BAS has five bases all manned throughout the year, and South Georgia is one of them. It was vital that I got not only permission but also the cooperation of BAS because I knew their vast experience of the area would be vital.

When I first approached the BAS Director, Dr Laws, it was obvious that he feared two women on their own would be unable to cope with the very difficult conditions on the island. One of his main worries was that BAS members might be called away from their survey work to help us if we got into difficulties. We managed to allay these fears – we had, after all, already spent some months on an uninhabited island and, although the conditions on South Georgia were likely to be much more severe, Annie and I had agreed between ourselves to be extra careful.

In fact, when permission was granted – at the eleventh hour – BAS proved to be generous in the extreme not only making one of their huts available to us, but also agreeing to transport all our equipment out on one of their survey ships, the Royal Research Ship, *John Biscoe*. We had a lot more specialist equipment and clothes to take with us than on previous trips. The temperature on South Georgia rarely rises more than a couple of degrees above freezing and the constant wind and sea turbulence meant we had to be prepared for anything. Our equipment included polar sleeping bags, snow goggles, thermal underwear and something that was to prove invaluable – a solar panel.

The *Biscoe* had sailed from Southampton with all our gear on board while Annie and I had flown out to join the ship at Rio de Janeiro and on 5 October 1981, we stood on the deck happy to be, at last, on our way, though not too happy with the hot stickiness of Rio and the vile smells which hung on the still air in the harbour. Two days later, the *Biscoe* slipped her moorings and slid gently out of the harbour running us into a fresh breeze which helped to dispel some of the stink and sweat.

On the third day we hit our first gale. Coming from the south-west at fifty knots, it created twenty-foot waves that broke in a thunderous roar over the bow of the ship and cascaded along the poop deck. The wind lasted for two days and cut our speed to seven knots. After a week at sea, we crossed the point where the icy waters of the Antarctic meet the warmer waters of the north, known as the Antarctic Convergence. Entering the area is as momentous as crossing the Equator. It was at this time that a chill began to settle. It was also about this time that we noticed the birds starting to follow the ship – birds we had never seen before – cape pigeons, wandering albatross, the grey-headed albatross, and several kinds of Antarctic petrels. We also saw a minkie whale. These animals are about twenty feet long and are still hunted by the Japanese. The minkie played with the ship for half an hour, surfacing alongside and then diving underneath the keel. Looking at this little whale, I found it impossible to understand how any human being with any feeling could fire an explosive harpoon into such a creature.

After nine days' sailing, we reached Bird Island on the north-west tip of South Georgia. The original intention had been to drop off some of the BAS team here but a hundred-mph gale developed, whipping up a storm of snow and ice which came driving at us horizontally, almost ripping the skin off our faces and making landing impossible. For six hours we sailed up and down into the wind and by lunchtime the visibility had improved and we could see Bird Island clearly, as well as part of the South Georgia mainland. Being early spring, the land was still covered in snow, giving it an appearance both beautiful and imposing.

After lunch, the wind began to ease and the *Biscoe* slid into Bird Sound. Rubber boats were lowered and the team quickly taken ashore. Most of their equipment, including food, was already at the camp, left there since last summer. Two hours later, the *Biscoe* pulled up her anchor and started to ease her way down to Grytviken, her next destination on the east coast of South Georgia. I had an important pilgrimage to make in Grytviken – to the graveside of a very great man.

South Georgia was described by Sir Ernest Shackleton as 'The Gateway to the Antarctic'. It is a tiny speck of an island lying on the edge of the most desolate part of the world. Freezing and snowbound, it is battered mercilessly by the Roaring Forties. South Georgia is one of the peaks of the vast submerged mountain range that runs from Chile almost to the Pole itself. It was because of the terrifying storms whipped up by the Roaring Forties that seafarers, and whalers in particular, were forced to seek shelter among the many deep bays and fjords which lie along the east side of the island.

Despite the ever-moving seas and the relentless turbulence of the air, South Georgia, at times, can be an island of incredible beauty. The towering snow peaks sparkle and glisten, dominated by Mount Paget, at 9,565 feet the tallest in the range. The glaciers dazzle the eye with their brilliance as they pour down to the sea, wedged tight between the mountains.

Northerly winds bring most of the bad weather. When passing warmer waters to the north, the winds become laden with moisture which condenses on reaching the colder atmosphere of South Georgia. Southerly winds blowing from the Antarctic continent usually bring dry, clear but very cold weather. Because of this the south-east end of South Georgia gets much clearer weather than the north-west end. The prevailing north-westerly winds lose their moisture during their progress down the length of the island. It is amazing that Edinburgh, which lies in the corresponding latitude in the north as South Georgia in the south, should be so different in climate and habitat. This is because Britain enjoys the warm waters of the Gulf Stream.

Plant life is not found in any great abundance. Tussock grass covers much of the low-lying ground up to about five hundred feet, then the covering consists mainly of mosses, lichens and liverworts. Kelp can be found in large quantities along the coast.

In 1775 Captain Cook landed on the island in search of the west coast of the 'Gulf of San Sebastian' which was supposed to separate the mythical Southern Continent from the known continent of South America. On his journey round the coastline, he discovered he had found not a continent but merely an island and he named one of the headlands Cape Disappointment, claiming the whole island for Britain and naming it after George III.

With the news brought back by Cook of the abundant wildlife to be found on South Georgia, it wasn't long before man turned up to slaughter fur seals for their skin and the elephant seals and penguins for their oil. The exploitation of South Georgia by British and American sealers had begun. Ships anchored in the small bays while the crew went ashore to set up the huge pots for boiling down the seal blubber. They were followed by new gangs who moved remorselessly along the shore clubbing the basking seals to death. A few quick strokes with sharp knives and the carcasses were stripped of their blubber and left to rot. When they had killed all the seals in one bay, they moved on to the next.

By 1823, it was estimated that 1,200,000 fur seals had been killed. Elephant seals were hunted because they carried a thick layer of blubber beneath their skin from which valuable oil was extracted. The sealers were unbelievably brutal to the bull elephant seals, driving them from the harems down to the water's edge, so that when they were shot and stripped of their blubber the men didn't have far to haul their heavy loads to the boats. Any bulls who showed a reluctance to leave their harems were beaten ferociously. Impatient to get the bulls down to the water, the whalers would batter them with long poles, sometimes accidentally knocking out an eye in the process. Iron bars were pushed down their throats when the bulls reared up to roar, resulting in broken jaws and splintered teeth. Much of the injury to the bulls was caused not by intent but by the whalers' desire to get the job over and done with. Once dead, the ends of the seals' tail flippers were cut off and hooks embedded in the stump for winching. The slaughter continued – seal pups were clubbed to death and bulls shot – and the animals were in grave danger of extinction.

It was the whale trade, however, that fixed South Georgia firmly on the map, luring hundreds of tough men from all over the world in search of easy money. The island became the centre of the southern whaling industry.

From May to October, whales bask in the warm waters of the north, concerned only with mating and family life. They eat nothing during these five months. When the giant babies are strong enough to travel, the whales turn south to their feeding grounds. The Antarctic sea is rich in krill and plankton, a diet on which the whales soon grow fat. The whales feed from the surface to a depth of fifty fathoms surging forwards, with mouths open, taking a ton of krill with each mouthful. They feed continuously day and night for seven months.

Whalebone was used in the construction of corsets or for any stiffening required in female garments. It was also used as the framework of umbrellas and parasols and even in carriage springs. Whalebone is not bone but part of the whale's skin and acts as a strainer in the animal's mouth. The whales swim along with their mouths open, krill and water pouring in. When the mouth is full, it closes and the water is forced out at the corners, the baleen plates or whalebone acting as a sieve to keep the krill in.

The early whalers went after the smaller variety of whales, the 'right' and sperm whales. In those days, catching whales was done by hand. A boat was rowed alongside the whale and the harpoon thrown into the back of the animal. There was nothing the crew of the boat could do except wait for the whale to stop towing them around the South Atlantic from sheer exhaustion. Then the crew would stab the exhausted animal to death with long lances. In those early days there were so many whales in the area that there was no need to go out into the open sea, and sperm and humpbacks were hunted within Cumberland Bay.

In 1904, the Swedish Antarctic Expedition arrived to explore the island. Near Cumberland Bay the expedition found some sealers' pots — used for boiling down blubber — and named the place Grytviken or 'Pot Cove'. Captaining the expedition ship was C. A. Larsen, who later returned to set up a whaling station at Grytviken. By 1912, another six stations had been established, including Stromness and Leith. With so much activity going on, a Resident Magistrate was appointed by the Government of the Falkland Islands, as South Georgia was by now part of its dependencies. Svend Foyn, a Norwegian, was the first man to use a harpoon gun which fired a heavy cast-iron harpoon with an explosive head. Steam ships were introduced to chase the larger species.

Not surprisingly, the whales couldn't survive this appalling massacre for much longer and, later, the introduction of the helicopter for spotting whales from the air was the final act of brutality. The machine, linked by radio to the whaler, can spot, follow and hover over the victim. It is probably the agonising death of the whale that particularly troubles people. The first harpoon rarely kills and often anything up to six are needed before the whale's despairing fight is over and it meets its convulsive death. *When* will man learn? Some international controls have been introduced and the last whaling season in South Georgia was in 1962. Britain sold her whaling fleet in 1963 and now Japan and Russia are the only nations to continue whaling.

South Georgia, however, is probably better known for its connection with Sir Ernest Shackleton. In 1914, Shackleton wanted to cross the Antarctic continent, the first time it was ever to be attempted in honour of Britain. One of the two vessels used, the *Endurance*, predecessor to the present naval ice ship, was to land on the coast of the Weddell Sea where Shackleton and his party would cross the continent, via the Pole, to the Ross Sea, eighteen hundred miles away. The second vessel, the *Aurora*, went to the Ross Sea and deposited food supplies at various locations inland for the trans-continental party to use as they made the latter part of their journey.

The *Endurance* battled her way south through the ice until, with summer gone and winter starting, she became firmly stuck in the ice. For eight months, she lay trapped until eventually she was crushed by the pressure of the pack ice. Shackleton and his twenty-five men abandoned her and eventually took to an ice floe where they lived for five months, feeding mainly on seals and penguins. They had with them the three life boats from *Endurance*. During those five months, the men did in fact sight land several times, but the ice was too broken up to walk over and not open enough to use the boats, so they had no alternative but to watch helplessly from their ice floe as they drifted by. On 9 April 1915, an increasing swell (indicating they were nearing the edge of the pack ice) broke up their ice floe and at last they were able to launch the three life boats.

For six days, Shackleton and his men rowed, sailed and baled out their boats, which were heavily laden and constantly shipping water. The men were soaked to the skin in temperatures well below freezing. Finally, they landed on the uninhabited Elephant Island. For the first time in fourteen months, the men stood on firm ground. With winter again approaching and food supplies limited to seals and penguins, Shackleton decided to sail to South Georgia, eight hundred miles away, using their twenty-two-foot open boat. The Falkland Islands were nearer, but the prevailing westerly winds would not have allowed him to reach them.

Shackleton with five of his companions set sail on 26 April 1916, leaving the other men on the island. For sixteen days they had hardly any sleep and very little hot food. During one gale, ice which had formed all over the boat had to be hacked away. On 9 May, six near-dead men entered King Haakon Bay. However, King Haakon Bay is on the south-western coast of South Georgia, whereas the whaling stations were all situated on the north-eastern coast. Shackleton knew that neither his men nor the boat were capable of the one hundred and fifty miles still to go. So he decided to climb over the island, something no one had ever done before.

For a few days, they all rested from the terrible journey, eating young albatross, penguins and elephant seals. Shackleton took two men with him to cross the island. The three men left King Haakon Bay in the middle of a clear night with a full moon. The interior was tremendously broken with high peaks, cliffs, glaciers and snow slopes. After thirty-six hours of continuous walking, they finally spied a trawler entering Stromness Bay, two thousand feet below them. Shackleton and his men had not been able to wash or cut their hair for over a year and when they finally climbed down to the whaling station the first people to see them were two young boys who looked at them with horror and then ran away.

Shackleton's first attempt to rescue his men left behind on Elephant Island was almost successful but he was forced back by the ice when he was within seventy miles of his goal. It wasn't until the fourth attempt that he managed to get through and bring help to his men, four and a half months after he had first left them. It is a tribute to his skill and leadership that throughout this terrible expedition he lost not a single man.

Shackleton returned to South Georgia in 1922, this time in a small ship called the *Quest*. By now, however, he was a sick man and on 5 January 1923 he died and was buried at Grytviken graveyard.

Now, steaming towards Grytviken nearly sixty years later, one of the first things I knew I had to do was to visit the grave of this great explorer. Annie and I were up by four the next morning to watch the island slip alongside us as we made our way into Grytviken. It was a beautiful morning, the sun shining and the sea calm and for the first time we were able to take a good look and see what we had let ourselves in for. We passed one huge glacier, called Fortuna, which plunged right down to the sea; it was several hundred feet thick when it was stopped by the water. It was a true glacier, with the ice-cold blue showing through in patches. We finally turned in to Cumberland Bay East and gently eased up to King Edward Point, also known as Grytviken base camp.

We stood on the bridge of the *John Biscoe* and watched the base camp come in to sight. It was an emotional moment as two small rubber boats full of men came roaring out to meet us. They whizzed round and round the ship, waving, shouting and laughing at us, all obviously thrilled to see the ship. Twelve men had been totally cut off at the base camp for six months and the *Biscoe* was the first ship of the summer season.

Letting off three blasts on her foghorn in reply to all their waving and shouting, she very carefully approached the small wooden jetty and the men scurried about securing the mooring lines. Eventually the gangplank was lowered. We all knew that the first priority was for the men to receive their mail and read it, so for a while everyone relaxed waiting for the men to reappear and start the task of unloading all the supplies. Food, drink, snow tractors, matches, loo rolls and snow shoes were brought up out of the ship's hold and winched down on to the jetty.

The five British Antarctic Survey camps scattered about the Antarctic are at Signy Island, Faraday, Rothera, Halley Bay and South Georgia. The base at South Georgia was built in 1969 after the collapse of the whaling industry. During the winter, eight men live there, their number trebling in the summer. Their work consists mainly of ionospheric, biological and meteorological studies. BAS has two ice-strengthened ships which ply between the bases – the *John Biscoe*, which had brought us down to Grytviken, and the much larger *Bransfield*. There are also two ski-wheeled, twin-engined Otter aircraft which are used during the summer. These aircraft are used for radio echo-sounding of ice depths and for aeromagnetic surveys, as well as for the movement and supplies for field parties. BAS has its headquarters at Cambridge and three-way links between there, the ships and the bases are maintained by teleprinter via the Falkland Islands.

Grytviken base camp consists of a dozen small buildings and sheds and a large house called Shackleton House which serves as the living quarters for the men. Some of the sheds are used to store radio and meteorological equipment as well as food. Others are used as boat sheds and carpentry shops. We found a hundred or so elephant seals basking in the sun around the camp. These huge creatures are very docile and you can easily get to within ten feet of them. They lie about dreamily, their breath steaming in the cold air. Every so often they make a grunting noise, not unlike bath water gurgling down the waste. If you get too close, the animal will rear up towering over you and roar right down your ear in a display of ferocity which is frightening until you get used to it.

We walked a mile and a half round the bay to its head where the old whaling station of Grytviken still lies. This station was once a thriving little village, complete with a church, meeting hall, houses and a mass of store sheds and machinery shops. We had a marvellous time wandering round the station, although it was very hard and slow going owing to the fresh snow into which we sank thigh deep. The sheds were full of harpoon guns and heads, knives and a mass of other equipment, scattered all over the place. We saw the enormous ramps and winches that were used to winch up the massive whales. In one shed, I came face to face with a huge rat and beat a hasty retreat. Curiously, a lot of these rats have turned vegetarian now that no one lives there any more. Along the jetties lay three old steel whalers with massive funnels, quietly rusting and slowly being broken up by constant gales and storms.

Half a mile further on from the station, I stumbled on something wooden, deep down in the snow. It seemed to be a railing of some sort. Feeling my way round it, I realised it was an enclosure. I climbed inside and began my search. First, I found one grave stone and then another, and another, all dating back to the beginning of the century. Then I found what I was looking for. Emerging out of the snow was the top of what seemed to be a large headstone. Digging the snow away from the stone, I read the name – Ernest Henry Shackleton. I thought of the terrifying trek across snow and ice to Elephant Island and the death-defying journey he had made in an open boat across eight hundred miles of the world's most inhospitable waters – to end here in the peace and beauty of South Georgia. It was a proud moment for me to stand by the grave of this great man.

We spent two days at Grytviken going through all the equipment I was supposed to pick up and making sure it was loaded on to the *Biscoe*. The BAS base commander, Peter Witty, whom I had already met at the BAS headquarters at Cambridge, had made sure that all the supplies, camping equipment and fuel I needed were ready and waiting.

I had come to a number of financial arrangements with BAS which included buying a medical box from them on sale or return, as well as sledging boxes. These boxes contained a limited variety of carefully balanced food items – enough to provide nearly four thousand calories a day for twenty days. The list is reproduced overleaf. BAS also sold us some of their regulation winter clothing – moleskin trousers, one size too big so that we could get our thermal underwear on as well. These were the only things we knew would keep our legs warm. The other thing we hoped would keep us warm – inside this time – was the sherry and port which we were able to buy from the *Biscoe*'s food store.

On our last evening at Grytviken, the whole ship's company went up to Shackleton's House and we had a marvellous evening with the men. An incredible spread of food was set out on a twenty-foot-long dining-room table and drink flowed from the bar. Many of the men came to wish us a happy summer season at St Andrew's Bay. It was,

CONTENTS AND CALORIFIC VALUE OF BRITISH ANTARCTIC SURVEY
20 MAN/DAY SLEDGE RATION BOXES 1978 SPECIFICATION

Item	Quantity	Total calories
Ration biscuits	32 × 85 gram pkts	12784
Beef meat granules	10 sachets	4330
Mutton meat granules	10 sachets	4340
Curried meat granules	10 sachets	3710
Soups, assorted	10 × 1½ pint pkts	2610
Porridge oats (Mornflake)	2 × 500 gram tins	4050
Alpen (Muesli)	20 × 1½ oz pkts	3180
Milk powder	2 × 1 lb tins	4640
Potato powder	8 oz pkt	410
Butter	3 × 16 oz tins	10850
Cheese	2 × 12 oz tins	2590
Sugar cubes	3 × 500 gram pkts	5910
Slicing sausage	2 × 10½ oz tins	1995
Sardines	2 × 4 oz tins	672
Chocolate, milk	20 × 35 gram bars	4116
Chocolate, plain	20 × 35 gram bars	3808
Drinking chocolate	1 lb tin	1785
Tea	96 tea bags	–
Coffee	8 oz jar	–
Marmite	2 × 2 oz jars	–
Jam	1 × 2 lb tin	2350
Paste, meat & fish	4 × 2 oz jars	480
Dried onion	6 oz tin	130
Dried peas	8 oz pkt	224
Dried mixed vegetable	8 oz pkt	190
Curry powder	25 gram tin	59
Salt	25 gram tin	–
Pepper	25 gram tin	76
Multi-vitamin tablets	100 tablets	–
Can opener	2	–

Total calories: 75289

$$Calories\ per\ man/day = \frac{75289}{20} = 3764$$

after all, the first time that two women had come to South Georgia to work.

I went to bed that night tired and slightly apprehensive about setting off next day. We had spent only two days on South Georgia but that had been long enough to bring me face to face with the reality of what we were about to do. The rugged high-peaked mountains and the wild, barren desolation made me wonder how Annie and I would cope. Had I, perhaps, gone a bit too far this time?

7

HAREMS AND HUMANS

Early the next day, the *Biscoe* left Grytviken heading south for St Andrew's Bay. It had taken us nearly three weeks travelling from London to reach our filming location. The wind was blowing and it snowed heavily all day as our equipment was brought up on deck and loaded on the ship's launch, which was then winched down into the sea. Two rubber boats were also lowered and ten men scrambled down into them and roared off after the launch. Annie and I followed in a third boat to film as much of the activity as the blinding snow would allow. The launch anchored about one hundred yards off the beach while the little boats ferried the equipment from the launch to the beach. The men had to battle their way through thousands of elephant seals that packed the two-mile stretch of beach and then they had to push the last four hundred yards to the hut through knee-deep snow. The heavy equipment was loaded onto a sledge and pulled to the hut.

Tired and cold after the sea journey, I opened the door of the hut which BAS had kindly agreed to let us use. The hut – eight foot by twelve foot – was dark and full of boxes, boots and equipment left behind long ago by the previous occupants. Annie looked at me glumly and I knew she was finding it as hard as I was to imagine this as our home for the next six months. We returned to the beach and stood among the seals to wave goodbye to the *Biscoe*. It was now five o'clock and neither of us felt like doing anything about unpacking. I had just enough energy left to throw a tarpaulin over our supplies while Annie made up some soup. At first we were at a loss to know where to find water to cook and wash with until we realised we were surrounded by it. The only problem was – it was all frozen. We had to melt it first!

Without even washing or cleaning our teeth, we crawled into our sleeping bags and just before losing consciousness one dark thought crossed my mind. 'We must be mad,' I said to Annie, but she was already asleep.

Next morning, things looked brighter. The hut was long and narrow, divided into three rooms. The biggest one, in which we ate, worked and slept had two wooden bunks which took up half the space. There was a table and chair and in the kitchen area there were two primus stoves to cook on. The tiny cloakroom we used to store the cameras, boots and other equipment. We spent the next two days trying to turn the hut into a home. Boots, tools, sledging rations, bits of wood – they all came out while we scrubbed the inside of the hut. Using a pick-axe to cut through the snow and ice, we fixed up the radio aerial poles and a clothes line, and up on the roof I fixed my solar panel. I had invested £300 in the German-made panel and never regretted it as it went through the whole season without faltering. It trickle-charged down into a twelve-volt battery, to which, in turn, I attached my camera battery – no noise, no fuel, no expense. This was the furthest south a solar panel had ever been taken and I never had to do anything more than give it a good polish from time to time – and clear the snow off it, of course!

We used an empty forty-five-gallon drum as a rubbish bin and burnt the contents each week. The hut was so small that most of our equipment had to be stored in a depot which we stacked up against the outside of the hut. Here we put the main bulk of our food, fuel, trunks, camera cases, hides and tents. Our final laborious task was to melt down the snow for water – it took two hours to make five gallons.

For the first few weeks, the weather was bitterly cold and well below freezing. Thick snow lay everywhere and any part of the body that was not covered quickly suffered. When going out filming, we piled all the camera equipment on to the sledge, put on our balaclavas – Annie had brought a red one – and waterproof fur-lined boots and then struggled onto snow shoes. Armed with ski-sticks, we would each grab a rope of the sledge and set out for the penguins. The snow shoes made all the difference, stopping us from falling knee-deep into the snow. Although, at first, we had many a laugh as we wobbled about losing our balance and tripping over, eventually we got the knack of how to walk on them. Controlling the sledge was a different matter. It seemed to have a very definite mind of its own. I stepped out of the hut one morning to find Annie glaring in fury at it:

'This bloody thing will not go the way I want it to. Do you know – I haven't felt so infuriated since I was a small girl and my doll, Betsy, wouldn't do what I wanted her to?'

'What happened to Betsy?' I asked.

'I'll tell you what I did to Betsy,' said Annie, looking malevolently at the sledge, 'I twisted her head off and threw her away.'

You can't do that to a sledge, of course, but we compromised by giving it Betsy's ill-fated name.

St Andrew's Bay is a shallow bay about two miles long. The beach, which is raised from the constant pounding of the surf, is covered in slate-grey sand. Our hut was tucked under the shelter of Mount Skittle which gives protection from the prevailing westerly and northerly winds. The king penguin colony was towards the southern end of the bay about a mile from the hut. There are three glaciers running into St Andrew's Bay and the largest one, Cook Glacier, came right down to the beach. Some parts of it did not look like a glacier at all as it was covered by a stony surface called moraine. The stones on the surface had been swept down from the mountain by the movement of the glacier. In the middle was the Unnamed Glacier and the third, the Heaney Glacier, lay at the northern end, near our hut. The last two were dazzling bright. The whole bay was surrounded by high snowy peaks, the tallest being nearly eight thousand feet. There were no trees and what little vegetation was revealed, once the snow had melted, proved to be coarse grass which grew in clumps on the low-lying hills. The landscape was bleak and barren but, to me, very beautiful.

We had many gales during our six months at St Andrew's Bay. Very early one morning, at about five, I was awakened by a noise outside. Inside, the books were falling off shelves and the whole hut seemed to be trembling. The sharp noise had come from the flapping of the tarpaulin covering the depot; it seemed about to take off. Quickly, we struggled into our anoraks and boots. Outside, the eighty-five-mph wind nearly knocked us off our feet. We staggered about collecting as many heavy stones as we could find to weigh down the tarpaulin, blinded by the stinging snow which blew into our faces. Walking into the wind, we had to bend double to force our way forward and sometimes we crashed into the hut as we were carried forward almost out of control. We continued to gather stones as the raging wind seemed to tear our clothes off us. Finally, I decided we had gathered enough and that the tarpaulin looked fairly secure.

Usually, our alarm went off at six a.m. and I would be the first to get up and get dressed. It was impossible for both of us to dress at the same time, as there was not enough room, so while I made the tea, Annie got dressed. If it was a sunny day, we would wash a few clothes, but just a few things at a time. We had learned our lesson on the first wash day. It had been sunny but very cold and as soon as we hung the clothes on the line, everything went ramrod stiff, frozen solid to the line. Having done the washing, we would tidy up the hut, collect water and be ready to start filming by eight. If the weather held, we would not be back until six p.m.

During the day, a bar of chocolate and a few sweets would help keep the hunger pangs at bay. We had to use heavy face cream and lip salve as well as sun lotion to try to counteract the dreadful drying effect of the wind, which seemed to take the moisture out of everything. When we got back in the evening, Annie would start cooking supper while I would get on to Grytviken to let them know we were all right, using the radio telephone which BAS had kindly lent us. Supper was the same every night – for six months – meat granules, dried veg and powdered potatoes. Each sledging box would keep Annie and me going for several weeks. They included things like sausage meat, tea, sugar and Alpen and although it made a monotonous menu, it kept us warm and healthy and we never starved. After supper, I would unload and reload the film magazines and write up my notes and then we would settle down to listen to the World Service or maybe play a game of scrabble or backgammon. By nine, we would be ready to collapse into our bunks. I slept on the top bunk as Annie found it difficult to climb up and, even worse, found it hard to climb down again. This gave me a distinct advantage as the heat from the Tilley lamp made my bunk several degrees warmer than hers.

As the weather gradually became warmer, the snow and ice on the low-lying land and hills began to melt. A little fresh-water stream appeared near the hut which meant we didn't have to spend precious time melting snow to drink. We started to carry our things in the rucksacks, having cruelly abandoned Betsy the sledge, which was tied up to the hut ready for next autumn. Melt streams from the glaciers began to flow and as the thaw increased, so too did the amount of water. For a while, we were able to wade across these streams, but I remember one day when we crossed over the stream in the morning and found, on returning in the evening, that it had altered its course and was now too deep for us to cross. We could either walk back four miles and round by the glacier to the hut or we could strip and wade across the ten yards of water. I decided that the shallowest and least swift crossing point was where the melt stream flowed into the sea. We took off our boots, trousers and long johns and began to wade out. The water was thigh deep and within seconds the pain in my feet was agonising. It took about two minutes to get across and during that time, my feet and legs had gone a deep purple and were covered in tiny cuts from small bits of sharp ice that were in the water. Now that we knew it was possible, we had to go back a second and third time for the cameras and equipment!

I have already mentioned that when we arrived at St Andrew's Bay in October, the beach was packed with elephant seals. The elephant seal is by far the largest seal with a big bull measuring up to eighteen feet and weighing three tons. It has a thick layer of blubber beneath the skin which yields a high-grade oil and it is because of this that it was mercilessly slaughtered. By 1885, the elephant seal on South Georgia was virtually extinct. Of more recent times, however, it has been protected and numbers have been increasing.

The main feature of the elephant seal, apart from size, is the extraordinary appearance of the nose on the adult bulls — a proboscis which hangs down over the mouth. This can be inflated with air when the bull is under stress and especially when angry.

Elephant seals spend their Antarctic winter at sea, returning to their breeding grounds in late August. The bulls are the first to appear and begin staking out their territory. The females appear a few weeks later and the name of the game is for the bull to get as many cows as he can into his area. While the cows are ashore, the bulls fight continuously, roaring defiance and lumbering after any other bull who ventures too close. Lifting his head and raising his chest on his front flippers, with proboscis inflated, the bull opens his mouth and lets out a mighty roar. If the intruding bull does not back off then the owner of the harem will charge, quite oblivious of what may lie in his path. Both cows and pups may be squashed and tiny new-born pups are often crushed to death. When the two bulls meet, they rear up as high as they can, both flippers clear of the ground and then they lunge at each other trying to inflict neck wounds with their upper canine teeth. Sometimes, only the flat of their necks collide, with a resounding slap, and they try again. Although the fights do not last long, injuries do occur, ranging from small surface scratches to large areas of torn flesh. The defeated bull backs off and heads for the sea and the defending bull will immediately return to the harem to stand guard.

Pups are born in early October, weighing about eighty pounds and can treble their weight in three weeks. Squabbles inside the harem can also break out. A cow rolling onto her side to allow the pup to feed may jostle a neighbour who may object and snap back.

While ashore, the elephant seals fast, losing a great deal of weight but living off reserves of fat. When the pups are three weeks old, they are weaned from their mothers who are then mated by the owner of the harem before returning to sea. The motherless pups begin to gather in large groups away from the beach where they lie around, occasionally playing with each other in the shallow pools. For a further month they continue to grow, their black woolly coats moulting and changing to beautiful silver ones. By December, they begin to move down towards the sea and after a short while, they leave, now totally independent.

Once the females have left the beach, the bulls follow and stay at sea for a few months, fattening up. In February they return to shed their skin. This process can take up to six weeks and they will sometimes travel hundreds of yards from the shore to find a suitable resting place for their vast bodies. The skin comes off in large patches, starting with the shoulders and back, then the stomach and flippers and finally ending with the face and head. This undoubtedly causes them a great deal of irritation as they are forever scratching but by April it is all over and they can return to sea to disappear again for five months.

We had a wonderful time with the elephant seals. For our first month or so, while they lay in their thousands all along the beach, we filmed as much of their breeding behaviour as possible. It was a bit of a problem trying to get into the harems while the rushing around and quarrelling was going on as I was forever having to look over my shoulder to make sure a cow or a bull wasn't about to attack me – and that I had an escape route if they *did* decide to attack. So, while I was busy filming, Annie would be close behind me armed with a ski-stick defending my back.

The tiny new-born pups, covered in their black woolly coat, and with those large appealing eyes were suckled by their mothers and grew at an alarming rate but many of them died on the beach at quite an early age. Some were crushed by charging bulls, others lost their mothers when the cows got involved in a fight and couldn't find them afterwards. Sheathbills, skuas and giant petrels were always on patrol around the seething, groaning and grunting mass, edging nearer to the sick or the lost pups, waiting till they were too weak to keep their predators at bay. As soon as the bird knew the pup was too weak to defend itself, it would dive in, pecking at the soft warm body, going for the most vulnerable areas – the eyes and the stomach. For a little while, the pup would make pathetic efforts to ward off the birds but its movements would grow weaker until eventually it died. It did not take the scavengers long to

ABOVE   Sir Ernest Shackleton's memorial cross above the BAS base at Grytviken

RIGHT   Our hut at St Andrew's Bay when we first arrived in October 1981, with our equipment being unpacked and stored

PREVIOUS PAGE   One of the storms on the *John Biscoe* during our voyage south

ABOVE Wading
through the ice-cold
water at the mouth of
the Heaney Glacier
melt stream

LEFT Unpacking
the sledge to start
filming

LEFT Annie washing clothes outside the hut

CENTRE Filling the Tilley lamp with paraffin

BELOW *Front row L to R:* Mavis Hunt, Lt-Commander Mike Green, Naval Doctor Neil Munro, Rex Hunt; *back row L to R:* myself, Captain Nick Barker, during the first visit from *Endurance* in December 1981

OPPOSITE ABOVE The *John Biscoe* anchored beside the BAS base at Grytviken, October 1981

OPPOSITE BELOW The mass of elephant seals on the beach at St Andrew's Bay during October and November

ABOVE A pair of elephant seals. Note the enormous size difference between the bull and the cow. The bull is attempting to calm the female and mate with her

RIGHT Annie giving a young elephant seal pup a playful tickle

PREVIOUS PAGES Two bull elephant seals threatening each other

LEFT Sitting on a docile bull elephant seal which is shedding its skin

BELOW A large bull elephant seal asleep on the beach, with some king penguins in the background

ABOVE A bull elephant seal flicking damp sand over its back to help it keep cool

RIGHT An elephant seal pup playing in a melt stream pool

Reindeer stag, with the king penguin colony in the background

ABOVE The two of us at the top of the tussock cliff checking on the three-month-old light-mantled sooty albatross chicks

LEFT An adult light mantled sooty albatross

OPPOSITE A king penguin calling outside the colony with its well-developed chick waiting to be fed

PREVIOUS PAGES
A pair of king
penguins at the
colony about to
change over egg
incubation duty

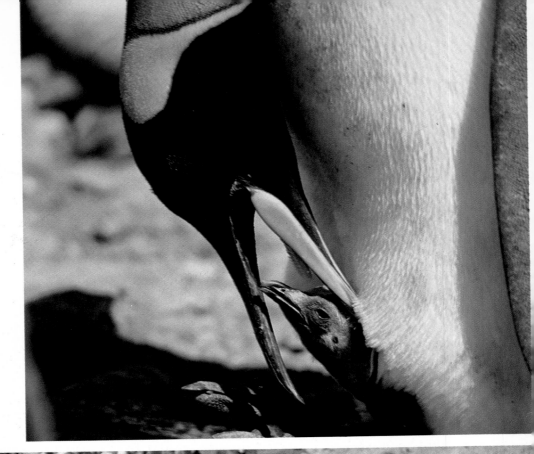

RIGHT A newly
hatched king
penguin chick being
fed

BELOW Filming in
the colony
surrounded by well-
grown, downy king
penguin chicks

strip the little body down to the bare bones which, after a while, were bleached to a gleaming white in the wind and sun.

The younger bulls, with no harem of their own, stayed as near as they dared. They would laze about in the melt streams, spending all day on their backs in the icy water with just the tip of their noses breaking the surface. Every now and then, they would sneak up quietly to the nearest cow and try to mate her. The cow would start bellowing and the owner of the harem would let out a terrible roar and charge the young bull, flattening everything in his path. Usually, the young bull would disentangle himself and make a dash back to the melt stream for safety. Occasionally he might stand his ground and if the battle went on for too long, blood might be drawn and flesh torn. Once, I saw a very large, old bull with half its proboscis hanging from its face by a thin thread of skin.

One day, we rather stupidly left our rucksacks on the beach while we filmed. Later, we found an enormous bull fast asleep on top of them. We grabbed his hind flippers, hoping he would move forwards but he simply flipped them violently, sending us spinning down the beach. Eventually we had to get down on our hands and knees and feel about underneath for the squashed rucksacks which we finally managed to heave out.

Recording the bulls and cows turned out to be rather amusing. Annie had the job of getting as close as she could to the bulls with the microphone while I sat nearby with the recording equipment making sure the levels were right. I admired Annie greatly because although the huge bulls reared up beside her, roaring down the microphone, never did she desert her post. As she weaved her way in and out of the seals, the cable would get itself entangled with the pups and cows and some of the pups would play with it, grabbing it in their mouths.

By mid-November, the pups had been weaned and they would often go to play in the many deep pools nearby. A mischievous pup would swim up to another one which might be lazily floating on its back and suddenly seize a front flipper. The two would roll over together in the water, making their curious dog-like barking calls.

We had noticed that on warm, sunny days, the seals lying on the beach would flick sand onto their backs, using their flippers. This helped to keep them cool. I decided to help one particular young pup who was snoozing in the sun and, grabbing a large handful of sand, I sprinkled it over his back. He opened one eye, snorted and then closed it again. Encouraged, I scratched his back and under his chin. He liked this and sniffed my arm, pressing his nose into my jersey. He then stretched over and pressed his face right into mine and, as I lay quietly beside him, suddenly, with no warning, he blew his nose straight at me. Annie, who was filming all this, fell about laughing but the pup just closed his eyes again and went to sleep.

Our hut area proved a favourite haunt for the pups as they liked to sniff around the fuel drums and play in the stream nearby, but we had to drive them away as they turned the water – which we drank – into a thick, muddy soup. Reluctantly, we would shoo them away with our ski-sticks but it wouldn't be long before they were back again.

One night, Annie had to get up to answer a call of nature and I was awoken by the noise of her swearing, followed by a lot of grunting and snorting which I was sure wasn't Annie. Grabbing my torch, I saw her at the door trying to make an elephant seal back out of the hut. The seal had been asleep against the door and when Annie had opened it, in he had flopped, each startling the other. On another occasion, I found a large cow fast asleep with her head inside our rubbish bin.

By the middle of January, young bulls and cows had started to return to St Andrew's Bay to shed their year-old skin for a new one. The old skin begins to peel and they spend a lot of time rubbing up against the tussock clumps and wallowing in the stinking mud pools. On days when the winds blew in from the sea, the smell of them was almost too much to bear.

The big bulls came ashore to shed their skin in February. I wanted to film the shedding skin so we went down to the beach where Annie filmed me creeping up to the huge sleeping bulls and peeling off large patches of skin. Without realising it, I had chosen a very docile bull and when I scratched his back his only reaction was to raise his head, give a sigh and go back to sleep.

I decided to get some fun photographs, so with a quick sign of the cross I very slowly lowered my backside onto the bull and, crossing my legs, tried to look as relaxed as possible while Annie clicked away with her camera. The bull still paid no attention to me so I climbed up onto his back and sat astride him. Annie then had a go and then we decided to film it all over again. Once we had got all we wanted I began climbing down off the bull and was just swinging my legs over the back to slide down when he suddenly heaved and snorted, causing me to lose my balance so that I landed in a heap on the sand beside him. This in turn gave the bull a fright and he reared up and roared at me, so I beat a hasty retreat.

Elephant seals are not the most beautiful or delicate of creatures but they have a lot of character. Their wonderful facial expressions and their amazing grunts and groans made me feel very affectionate towards them. They are not the sort of animal you would like to cuddle and at first they can be a bit frightening because of their massive size. On the whole, however, they are very docile and they gave Annie and me many hours of enjoyment.

One Saturday towards the end of November we struggled out of bed at five a.m. to have a look at the weather. I had wanted to begin filming early but it was cloudy and dull so we went back to bed. Later, while still half asleep I heard vague noises outside the hut – first something at the door and then a tapping noise at the window followed by what sounded like human voices. I prodded Annie in the bunk below. 'Wake up,' I whispered. 'It's the Russians.' We'd seen their trawlers and factory ships pass down the coast. 'But they're talking English,' whispered Annie sensibly – and indeed they were. Cautiously I opened the door and there stood three members of the BAS team come to visit us on the *John Biscoe* from Grytviken. They had brought eggs and mail and while Annie made coffee for everyone, I rushed around gathering up three parcels of film that were to be taken for forwarding to London. Unfortunately they only stayed a short while. We walked down to the beach with them and helped to launch the two boats that would take them back to the *Biscoe*. Back in the hut, we had a pleasant hour going through the mail they had brought, our first for two months. Needless to say, the news that the girls had been caught in bed spread round South Georgia by radio in five minutes flat.

Our next group of visitors, one month later, gave us plenty of warning. HMS *Endurance*, the naval ice-patrol ship was due to bring the Governor of the Falklands, Rex Hunt, and his wife, on a visit. We knew Nick Barker, the Captain, from last season, when *Endurance* had come to Carcass Island to collect all our equipment at the end of the filming. Apart from bringing Rex Hunt on his tour, *Endurance* also had on board sixteen men belonging to the Joint Services Expedition who were going to climb some glaciers and do some scientific work. Their base camp was at Royal Bay, ten miles south of us. (Little did we realise at the time that we would one day spend a night with two of them in a tiny tent.) The plan was that the Hunts would fly to us by helicopter and spend the day here while *Endurance* unloaded all the equipment belonging to the expedition. We were invited on board for dinner and would be flown back to St Andrew's Bay the following day. Two days before their arrival, we turned our depot upside down looking for some smart clothes to wear. Then we had to pack up exposed film to be taken back for forwarding to London. My filming notes had to be typed up, last-minute letters written, hair washed, rubbish burned and the hut cleaned out – ready for our visitors.

Saturday, 12 December – the day they were expected – was a day of great excitement, though it was also to bring some unexpected drama that we could well have done without. I put up the Union Jack – a gift from my local pub in Norfolk. The flag was in honour of Rex Hunt, but would also serve as a wind indicator for the helicopter pilot. The helicopter from *Endurance* came straight in and hovered about fifty feet up and I could see Rex waving from the open door. Tilting its head, the helicopter began a slow gentle descent. Something, however, seemed to be wrong and I realised, to my horror, that the machine was continuing to lose height. It hit the ground hard and as it bounced forward on its nose, the rotor blades sliced through the entire tail section, cutting it off from the main body of the helicopter which finally rolled over on its side and came to rest.

Rotor blades and bits of metal flew all over the place though thankfully nothing hit either us or the hut. For a moment, there was a frightening stillness and then I thought, Fire! and rushed back to the hut to grab a couple of fire extinguishers. We ran to the helicopter to find the four occupants climbing out, alive and safe. The engine was still smoking and we all backed away to a safe distance, still feeling the shock. Relieved, we greeted Rex and Mavis and took the pilot back to the hut so that he could radio a message to *Endurance*. While we were all having a stiff drink, the second helicopter flew over from the ship and landed safely. It seemed that the whole thing had been due to pilot error. The wind at Royal Bay had been blowing from the north-west, at about forty knots, coming down off the glaciers. At St Andrew's Bay it was blowing at fifteen knots, but from the north-east. The pilot saw the flag flying but did not register that the wind was blowing in a different direction.

Restored by the drink, Rex and Mavis set out with us to see the elephant seals and it wasn't long before we were all chatting away and laughing again. At 6.30 p.m., *Endurance* appeared on the horizon steaming towards us. The second helicopter returned and took Rex and Mavis back to the ship and then returned for us. We had an absolutely marvellous time on *Endurance*, where we slept in the sick bay. We were delighted to find a shower which we used at every opportunity. We changed into our skirts, put on a little make-up and joined Nick Barker and all the other officers in the Wardroom for a fantastic buffet supper. Annie and I made complete pigs of ourselves. Smoked mackerel, followed by steak and then fresh fruit salad. It beat our dehydrated meat granules any day! Finally, we stumbled to the sick bay at two a.m., escorted to the door by at least three officers.

For the next two days, *Endurance* stayed close at hand, spending the day at Royal Bay, continuing to off-load all the stores and equipment for the Joint Services Expedition, and then sailing back to St Andrew's Bay for the night. Each evening, a boat would land on the beach and take us back to the ship for the night. Five mechanics came ashore on the second day and spent the whole day dismantling the crashed helicopter and on the following day the second machine was able to fly the remnants back to the ship in a huge net that hung underneath it.

For two days, we showed as many people as possible round the bay until we were quite exhausted. After two months of living quiet and peaceful lives, we found that three days of drama, excitement and activity, along with good food, drink and late nights on board, were as much as we could take. Even the penguins and seals were rather startled and confused by it all. Never had they seen anything like it. People milling about all over the place and everybody wanting to take photographs of them. Finally, early on Tuesday morning, with a thick fog reducing visibility to under one hundred yards, a boat took Annie and me back to the beach and left us there. We were exhausted, with huge black circles under our eyes. We stumbled over the rocky flat land for four hundred yards back to our hut, dragging our skirts and shirts along the ground behind us. On reaching our hut, we collapsed onto our bunks. Oh God, did we feel awful? We unpacked our bits and pieces, sorted out the hut, did some washing, had some lunch and then went to bed and slept the entire afternoon.

Next day, we sorted out the goodies which *Endurance* had brought from England. Christmas was only ten days away and our families had sent parcels which we dutifully hid away for Christmas Day. *Endurance*'s own gift to us was one of a very practical nature. Back in England, I had said to Nick that one of the things I would miss at St Andrew's Bay was not being able to sit on a loo and he had got the ship's carpenter to make us one! It was a square box with canvas sides and a very comfortable padded backrest so that we could lean back and enjoy the scenery. Our bucket fitted neatly inside and there was a tall pole fixed to the back of the box with a chain and handle dangling from it, just like an old-fashioned loo. Screwed to the pole was a holder for the loo roll and a hook in case we ran out of paper – we'd even been given bits of torn newspaper to use – *The Times*, of course. When we tried out the loo for the first time, we found that it had been built for men of six feet and not for ladies of five foot four. We found our feet dangling in the air. That was no problem, however. I got out the saw and cut off three inches from each leg and we were then comfortable. In fact, our morning sessions were often the highlight of the day!

When we had arrived at St Andrew's Bay, the albatross had already gone through the main part of their courtship display although I did manage to film some immature birds practising for next season. The light-mantled sooty albatross weighs about six pounds, stands two feet high has a wing span of six or seven feet. It has a dark grey head with a pale blue stripe along the lower mandible and its feet are a pale grey. The most striking feature is a startling white arc over the eye which gives the bird the appearance of being constantly surprised. Its call is a sort of wail, a woeful sound which sent a chill down our spines when we first heard it.

Once a pair are together, they circle each other, tail feathers fanned out, stamping their flat feet on the ground and fencing with their beaks. Every now and then, they break off with one of their eerie calls, starting with their heads and necks fully stretched pointing to the sky and ending with the head bowed. They also had a curious beckoning motion to each other as though to say 'come here'. Their nests, on the steep tussock-covered cliffs, were raised a foot or so above the ground and were made of mud and vegetation. The albatross at St Andrew's Bay used dead tussock grass leaves.

To our joy, on 29 October, we found the first large white egg. They only lay one which takes sixty-three to seventy days to incubate. The pair share the incubation period. They feed mainly on squid, small fish and krill. By 14 November all eight nests had eggs. The birds were very tame and would allow me to approach to within a few feet. Occasionally, I managed to put out my hand and stroke their backs and necks without the birds showing any sign of unease. During the nine weeks or so of incubation, I filmed the adults on their high mud nests rolling the egg or rearranging and collecting more nesting material. The sitting bird would grab a beakful of tussock grass growing by the nest and, by twisting and tugging at the grass, break it off and then arrange it in the nest. A great deal of time was spent sleeping on the nest. The only real sign of activity was when another albatross flew over the colony. This usually caused one or more of the sitting birds to start calling and often the flying albatross would land beside one of the calling birds. They were obviously a pair and change of duty would take place. After a few minutes of greeting and nibbling at each other's beaks, the sitting bird would get up off the nest and the other one would climb up onto it. The relieved bird would then plod to the edge of the cliff and fly off.

In late December, we found the first few eggs just beginning to pip. When we picked up the eggs and held them to our ears, we could hear the chick inside squeaking. It wasn't for another four days that the first egg hatched and we found a tiny bundle of pale grey fluffy down lying warm and snug underneath the adult. When hungry, the chick started to move around underneath its parent and squeak for food. The adult would then regurgitate digested food for the chick to feed on. The chick grew very rapidly and when only three weeks old was left quite alone at the nest. It was covered in long grey down except round the eyes and face, which were covered in a short white down which made it look as though it was wearing a huge pair of flying goggles.

During the summer, sadly, two chicks died, one, I feel certain, of over-heating. We had a very hot week in late January when the sun shone from a cloudless sky and a breeze blew so lightly, it barely rustled the grass. The chicks, covered in their thick down, had an awful time in the unaccustomed heat, panting heavily during the seven hours during which the colony was in the full glare of the sun.

The second chick died when it was seven weeks old. I had filmed it being fed by its parents, so starvation was not the cause of death. One morning, I was a little startled when a skua burst out of the thick tussock grass right by my face as I climbed up the steep cliff. I dug about in the grass and found a half-eaten chick. Checking the nests, I soon discovered which one it was. I think the skua must have attacked the chick on its nest and killed it. Whenever we approached the chicks, they would sit up and clap their beaks at us as a warning not to come any nearer and if we did go closer, we ran the risk of being squirted with a bright orange, foul-smelling, oily liquid that the chicks regurgitated from their stomachs.

The chicks sat quietly in their nests looking like woolly toys, panting on warm days and suffering in the bitter cold when it rained or snowed. Out of the eight nests, we watched seven chicks hatch. The eighth egg never hatched and of the seven chicks, five of them had reached their fledgling stage by the time we left in May. It wasn't until the chicks were nine weeks old that we saw the first sign of moulting of the baby down. The wings were the first to go, dark grey feathers replacing the pale grey down. When the wind blew and ruffled the fluffy down on their chests, we could see the feathers underneath, nearly ready to push the down out.

One particular chick was very much friendlier than any of the others, probably because I filmed it the most as its nest was the most accessible for the tripod and camera. One lovely sunny morning while I was sitting by this chick's nest waiting to film the adult flying in to the colony to feed its chick, the chick suddenly reached over and started to nibble at my trouser leg. I edged nearer and sat down right beside it and watched in amusement as it had a tug-of-war game with my shirt collar and gently preened my hair. It allowed me to stroke it and to bury a finger deep into its down where it was lovely and warm.

When the weather began to grow colder and the winds blew stronger we could see the chicks standing up and leaning slightly into the wind, stretching out their well-developed wings and starting to flap them. Just like the black-browed albatross in the Falkland Islands, the light-mantled sooty albatross chicks were exercising their wing muscles and practising for the day when they would bravely step to the edge of the cliff and launch themselves into space. Sadly, when Annie and I left, in early May, they were still practising and we never saw them leave, but we knew that in a few weeks' time they would be gone.

We had a very soft spot for the albatross. They were so graceful, gentle and beautiful. They could have flown away when we got close to them but instead they allowed us to run a finger gently down their backs and it was this trustfulness that made us love them just that little bit more.

8

KINGS OF THE ISLAND

When I began researching the wildlife on South Georgia, I found that it was rich in every variety – reindeer, elephant seals and albatross, which were present in large numbers, especially at St Andrew's Bay. The main reason, however, for selecting South Georgia as a filming location had been the presence there of the king penguin. When we arrived at St Andrew's Bay, we found ten thousand or so eleven-month-old chicks in the colony – the largest on South Georgia. To my mind, the king penguin is the most beautiful of the species. When standing erect, it is three feet tall. The head and neck are black with a dark green metallic area on the crown which gleams when caught in the sunlight. Just behind the ear and running to a thin line to the front of the throat is a startling orange mark, rather like a comma. At the top of the breast, the orange begins to fade to a pale yellow and gradually to a dazzling white down the front. The beak is black except for a pink stripe along the lower mandible. The eye is dark and the feet black and though both sexes have similar plumage, the male is slightly taller.

Kings walk upright with their flippers held slightly away from their sides and they take small, flat-footed steps. They have difficulty in getting over obstacles, even small stones, and often trip or fall. To get up again, they point their long slender beak into the ground and partially raise their body, then they use the tip of their flippers to push themselves fully erect again. If frightened, they will toboggan using the tip of their flippers and toes to propel themselves along the ground at quite a fast rate. Their two-inch tail feathers are used as a brush to sweep away debris when sitting in the colony and they are also used as a prop when sitting on their heels with toes pointing up in the air.

Their call which they make with the neck stretched to its limit and the beak pointing to the sky but closed, sounds like a bugle call. With flippers collapsed by its side, the chest heaves as air rushes in and out of the lungs. It makes several trumpeting calls, the last one ending with the head of the bird suddenly dropping right down so that the beak points to the ground. It holds this pose for a few seconds before relaxing. It is as though the bird is making a bow before an audience after a thrilling performance.

The breeding cycle of the king is rather complicated and lasts sixteen months. It is, therefore, impossible for a king to rear a chick annually. The best it can do is raise two chicks every three years. A pair of kings will breed early in the season of one short Antarctic summer. By the time the chick leaves the colony the following year, the pair will breed again, but this time much later in the summer. By the time the second chick is ready to go, it is then much too late in the season for the same pair to breed a third chick. So they miss out that season and are ready to start breeding again early in the following summer.

Breeding begins in October. Not yet paired, the kings come ashore, after a few weeks spent fattening up at sea. They do this because for the next four weeks they will have to go through a period of forced starvation, when they lose their old feathers and grow new ones. Moulting takes place *before* breeding, unlike most birds which moult *after* breeding. By the end of October, they have finished moulting and can return to sea for another few weeks to fatten up.

By mid-November, the kings come ashore again, in the prime of health, looking fat and sleek. This is the time when they pair up. Love is not always at first sight and it may take a while before they find a suitable partner. The pair starts to wander into the colony which is full of last season's young fluffy brown chicks. They force their way through the chicks, pushing them out of the way until they find a suitable site to start their courtship display. As more and more paired adults enter the colony, the chicks get pushed further and further out until they end up massing in thick groups on the fringes of the colony.

The adults then start their courtship. This involves strutting around in a small area, the male in the lead taking large exaggerated steps, the head swaying from side to side. If they go too close to another pair of displaying kings a short, sharp fight breaks out. Once the fight has blown over, the strutting, often in circles, continues until the two finally stop in a chosen spot and stand very close to each other with chests almost touching. They will stay there for quite long periods, gazing into each other's eyes, preening themselves and sometimes even having a short doze with their beaks tucked in behind their flippers. Every now and then, they suddenly become alert and stretch their necks up to the full limit, heads slightly bent to one side, and stay like that for as long as a minute, not uttering a sound. Slowly they both relax, their heads sinking back onto their bodies.

During the next stage, both birds make deep bows to each other uttering little clicking sounds with their beaks as they clap them gently. This obviously proves very exciting to the male in particular, as he starts to edge nearer to the female and while she is still making deep bows to the ground he puts his head and neck over the back of hers. They begin to shuffle round in tight little circles, the female's head still bent down and the male with his head pressing down on her bent neck. The male begins to exert a little pressure on the female to try to get her down on the ground. He starts to edge round to her back, his head still bent over the back of hers and places one foot on the base of her back as though he is trying to climb up it. The foot keeps slipping off but he perseveres and, at last, the female sinks to the ground lying on her front and raising up her short, stubby little tail. The male, with some difficulty because of his short legs, climbs up onto the back of the female, holding onto a few of her head feathers for support. He then gradually works his way backwards, his beak and flippers keeping him balanced until he comes up against the raised tail feathers of the female. He then lifts his tail feathers over those of the female, pressing down hard and mating takes place.

That is what should happen, but all too often the pair would be interrupted just at the wrong moment. Just when the pair was on the point of mating, a strange king would rudely barge in and start stabbing out at either the female or the hard-working male, destroying the romantic moment. How frustrating it must have been for them.

I found the first egg on 23 November. From then on the number increased daily. It was extremely difficult to know when a king was about to lay an egg. It is easy to see when they already have them. A large layer of skin folds down over the egg, which sits on their feet, covering the one white egg and keeping it warm. The bulge of skin and hunched attitude of the sitting bird is very noticeable.

Why do kings keep the egg on the top of their feet instead of building a nest? The only explanation I have come across and which seems feasible is the following: like their cousin the king, the emperor penguin also incubates the egg on the top of its feet. But the emperor breeds only on the Antarctic continent where there is no vegetation for nesting material. To lay an egg on the ice would be fatal as it would freeze in no time. This explains their habit of incubating their eggs on their feet. The king does exactly the same thing and although their colonies are not on ice, they are always near ice and snow. Perhaps long ago, kings lived in the same kind of environment as the emperor does today and habits die hard.

I was very lucky to witness and film a king actually laying an egg. Usually, when I walked through the colony the birds without eggs would move away to let me pass. Birds with the noticeable bulge would stand their ground, being able to shuffle along only at a very slow rate, otherwise the egg would drop off their feet. One day, I noticed a king who refused to move out of my way and yet who lacked the bulge that indicated an incubating egg. I thought that the bird was sick or injured and took a closer look at it. It looked all right, but still would not move. Then the bird heaved and it dawned on me that she was about to lay an egg! I set up my cameras and sat patiently waiting six feet away. Annie patrolled the surrounding area to prevent chicks and other adults from crossing in front of the camera or upsetting the star of the moment.

There was very little sign of effort as the female laid her egg. Every now and then she heaved and pushed down hard but remained standing all the time. Finally, from between her legs, the pointed end of the large white egg began to appear. Another push and more of the egg appeared. The camera never stopped rolling. A final push and the egg dropped down the few inches onto her feet. She immediately lowered her head and, using her beak, gently pushed the egg into a more comfortable position, then rolled the flap of skin down over the egg and her feet. She then relaxed, took on the hunched attitude and closed her eyes.

When the female has laid her one egg, she incubates it for a few hours and then lets the male take over. He comes up close to her while she unfolds the skin covering the egg and gently rolls the egg onto the ground. Immediately, he bends down and, using his beak, rolls the egg up onto his feet, folding his flap of skin back over the egg. The female then goes off to the sea to feed for two weeks while the male incubates the egg. When the female returns the egg is changed over and it is then the turn of the male to go off and feed, but only for about five days. Change over, from then on, takes place every five or six days.

It takes fifty-four or fifty-five days to incubate a king egg but within a matter of hours the spotless white egg is heavily stained from mud or muck on the ground. One would imagine that during the time of incubation, the colony would be relatively quiet and peaceful. This is not the case. Because the king does not use a nest but keeps the egg on its feet, the bird is able to move around, though very slowly. Kings like to be far enough apart from each other that when they stretch out their flippers fully they do not touch the next-door penguin. Therefore, when a king pushes past others to another place a fight will often break out.

With a scratchy, raucous sound they bash and stab at each other until they are so exhausted all they can manage to do is stand hunched over their eggs, puffing and panting, unable to continue the fight. With luck, it will end there and, eventually, the birds will quieten down, but often the fights go on much longer, ending up with blood drawn and even an egg being lost. Many times I saw an incubating bird trying to push past other sitting birds and immediately coming under attack. Naturally, the bird would fight back, but sometimes four or five birds would attack together. The king would get a terrible hiding, being stabbed and pecked by beaks from all sides, rocked by the blows, and with feathers plucked from its back. If the king is intelligent, it will lower its head, keep its balance using the tip of its flippers to touch the ground, continue to shuffle forwards with the egg still safely on its feet and break out of the fight it has caused.

However, it may get caught in a trap unable to go forwards, backwards or sidewards and surrounded by other kings intent on bashing and stabbing it so violently that the egg rolls off its feet. Then the only concern of the trapped penguin is to get the fallen egg safely back on its feet. Taking no notice of the awful thrashing it is receiving, it uses its beak to roll the egg back towards its feet. Sometimes it does succeed in rescuing the egg, but sometimes the king cannot get the egg back onto its feet and, in desperation, will abandon the egg and push through the fighting birds to find refuge in a more peaceful spot. Rarely does the bird attempt to find its lost egg. More often than not the sheathbills find it in a matter of minutes. They spend their day weaving in and out of the colony searching for abandoned eggs. They tap at the egg repeatedly with their short stubby beaks until the shell cracks, when they consume the contents.

There is a chance, if the parents were early breeders of the season, that they will mate again and lay another egg thus becoming late breeders.

It is rare to see a king hatching, as the egg is hidden from view under the fold of skin. The only telltale signs that hatching has taken place are fragments of the egg shell lying on the ground near a particular bird. I found such a bird on 20 January and sat down on some rocks nearby and waited.

Eventually, a tiny head, with eyes still tightly closed, peeked out from under the skin and squeaked. A newly hatched king penguin chick weighs about eight ounces and is blind and quite naked.

Filming the tiny chicks proved difficult. Because the outside temperature is fairly low, they spend a lot of time tucked away under the parent. On a warm, sunny day, they may come out for some fresh air, but, even then, the adult king will deliberately turn its back to the sun to protect the chick and this made my job of filming extremely frustrating. Very gently we would try to persuade the adult to turn and face the sun and perhaps just as I was ready to roll, another adult would walk in front of the camera and we would have to start all over again.

The adult will lower its head down to the chick and gently prod it with its beak, perhaps trying to push it back under the fold of skin. If the chick is hungry enough it will continue to squeak and beg for food. Sometimes more food comes out of the mouth of the adult than the tiny chick can cope with and part of the meal falls to the ground. The sheathbills, however, are waiting and dart in quickly to steal the fallen meal.

For the first week of the chick's life it is fed every four or five hours. After that, the periods between meals get longer and longer. Change-over duty between the male and female, once the chick is hatched, is approximately every five days as it was with the egg. The returning bird gets as close to the sitting bird as possible, chest to chest, and while peace reigns briefly around them, the sitting bird lifts up the fold of skin and allows its mate to pull the chick gently onto its own feet. The mate uses its beak to do this. The fold of skin folds down over the chick immediately.

The chicks grow extremely rapidly and after ten days they have a light covering of short brown down. They are still small enough to hide under their parents although they now appear far more frequently – either a head, a foot or a bottom poking out from under the fold of skin. They have more than doubled their weight to seventeen ounces. When they want to be fed, they come out from under their parents, stand by their feet, stretch up and squeak, begging for food. By the time they are two weeks old, the brown down has grown longer and become fluffier and they can no longer fit under their parents, although they do still try! The only part they manage to push in underneath the adult is their head leaving their fat, round bodies and large feet spread out behind them. The chicks now spend most of their time standing or lying beside their parents, preening their new down. At the first sign of nearby trouble, the chick will dive in under its parent, head only, to find safety and security.

140

One day, while I was filming some week-old chicks in the colony, I found a chick apparently abandoned, squeaking and calling for its parent. This tiny, naked chick was a pathetic sight, lost and frightened, surrounded by adults that pecked it if it got too near. I looked around to find its parent but without success. Keeping my eye on the lonely little chick during the day and shooing away the sheathbills, who almost certainly had nasty ideas, I continued filming. By the time I had finished filming, the little chick was still calling out for its parent and was tired and, no doubt, hungry. I couldn't leave it to be eaten by a sheathbill, so I started to examine the adults sitting nearby to find one that had a chick about the same age as the abandoned one. After a few minutes I discovered such a bird. Crawling on my hands and knees to avoid disturbing the colony too much, I gently picked up the lost chick and placed it before its new foster-parent, then I withdrew and sat down to wait. After a minute or two, the adult started to take an interest in the chick and shuffled forwards using its beak to push the chick on to its feet and under its fold of skin. It had a bit of trouble getting the chick onto its feet as there was already one occupant and little room to spare, but it managed and seemed quite content now with twins. I left the colony to return to the hut wondering if I had done the right thing or not.

Today, the king penguin colony at St Andrew's Bay is probably the largest on South Georgia. King penguins were first noted at St Andrew's Bay as far back as 1883. By early 1914, the colony was estimated to consist of thirty birds and by May 1925, the manager of the whaling station at Grytviken stated there were about eleven hundred king penguins. In 1926 this was considered to be one of the largest rookeries on the island. Counts made between the winter of 1972 and February 1974 revealed a total population of 6,000 to 7,500 birds including over 2,000 chicks. I personally never accurately counted the king penguins at St Andrew's Bay during the summer of 1981–2, but I am quite convinced that during the height of the breeding season, January and February, there were 50,000 king penguins scattered round the bay. This figure includes the breeding birds, the previous season's chicks and the non-breeding birds. I would estimate there were between 15,000 and 20,000 nests at the colony the year Annie and I filmed them.

Back in October, when the beach was packed with thousands of elephant seals, the kings had difficulty in weaving their way in and out of all the animals and always had to be ready to scatter should a massive bull flick his flippers at another bull. Parties of fifty kings, or more, coming from the colony would take hours to reach their launching rock, while they tiptoed through the mass of seals, trying not to disturb them. The kings would gather amongst the seals to try to find the best route out. They would then make a dash through a very narrow gap to reach the next little clearing.

We could never understand why the kings insisted on struggling along the beach, risking being flattened by the seals, when all they had to do was walk thirty yards further inland, away from the beach, where there were fewer seals. Then their journey from the colony to their launching rock would have taken a quarter of the time and would have been far less hazardous. But maybe this had been their route for countless years and therefore the only route they knew. We had quite a nerve-wracking time filming the kings weaving their way in and out of the seals as we ourselves had to get in amongst the seals to do so. Armed only with a ski-stick to fend off any aggressive bull or female, Annie would always stand behind me, while I was filming, to defend my back. Sometimes the seals would creep up slowly to within four or five feet of us and watch us at work.

Once the kings had succeeded in reaching the launching pad they would dive into the sea and stay away feeding for four or five days and on their return, laden with food, they would stop on the outside of the colony and call their chicks. If the chick were not within hearing range, the adult would enter into the mass of fluffy chicks and, after a few yards, stop and call again. Eventually, the chick would come running and start begging for food. Annie and I had countless amusing hours with these well-grown fluffy chicks. Once we had set up the camera and tripod, the chicks, full of curiosity, would slowly begin to move up to us. Thirty or forty of them would lean back on their heels and tails, their full stomachs bulging out in front of them, staring at us. If we moved slowly and carefully and stretched out a hand, the chicks would nibble our fingers. If we left our rucksacks unguarded while we went to look at something else in the colony, we would return to find several chicks with their heads inside the rucksacks, checking to see if there was anything they could play with.

Occasionally, the chicks' behaviour was just too friendly, especially when I wanted to get on with some serious filming. Often, when working in the colony, I would notice vibrations coming up through the tripod and the camera would shake very slightly. This usually meant that one or two chicks were pecking the legs of the tripod. Once, when I was filming an adult feeding its chick, an out-of-focus brown fluffy head filled the screen. It was a chick who had calmly walked round to the front of my camera and was staring down into the lens. Annie, who was photographing nearby, had to be Nanny. She walked a few yards from me and started to tap her ski-stick on the ground. The chicks who had gathered around me were attracted by the bouncing ski-stick and rushed over to Annie. She then had to keep them amused until I had finished filming.

Whenever we moved from one place in the colony to the other, a little band of chicks would follow. We would sometimes play Grandmother's Footsteps with them – whenever *we* stopped *they* would, and whenever we moved on they would follow.

During November, the fluffy chicks began to lose their baby down and they spent a great deal of time preening their new feathers. They would begin to move away from the colony, down to the beach or the ice-cold pools formed by the numerous glacier melt streams. This would be their first introduction to water. The chicks on the beach would have a rather frightening first experience as the surf exploded along the shore. They would creep down the beach to the point where they met the sea, bending down to nibble at the water as it lapped round their feet. Every now and then, there would be an extra large wave and the startled chicks would find themselves deep in white, foaming water. Thoroughly alarmed, they would race back to the security of the colony, puffing and panting, their fluffy down soaked and plastered to their bodies. After a while, they would start to creep back down to the beach again. The chicks playing in the quiet glacier melt pools were quite safe, so long as they didn't enter the melt streams. We could not cross these streams ourselves as they were far too deep and swift. Of course, every now and then a chick would fall accidentally into a melt stream and it would be swept down towards the sea at an alarming rate, bobbing up and down on the surface with a very surprised expression on its face. It would, eventually, struggle to the side and scramble out, looking very sad, with ice-cold water dripping from its sodden down. It would then spend hours preening itself and drying out.

Once, I had to rescue a chick who had accidentally fallen into the Cook Glacier melt stream that runs down one side of the colony. The sodden chick had managed to struggle onto a tiny ledge under the sheer melt stream bank, but was trapped as it could neither climb up the bank nor did it dare jump off the ledge into the deep and very swift current. The little creature was soaked through and shivering with cold, so I put down my cameras and, crossing over to the colony side of the melt stream via the glacier, waded out into the water. Clutching hold of the sheer bank, I was in constant danger of being swept clean off my feet as the melt water swirled round my thighs. I got a hell of a beating when I reached down and picked up the sodden chick. It stabbed out viciously with its sharp beak, but, luckily, I was wearing my thick down-filled jacket which took most of the beating. It then hammered me with its flippers and this I most certainly did feel, even through my jacket. I tucked the struggling chick under one arm and, keeping a very tight grip on it, turned round and began the very slow struggle back up the melt stream, until we reached dry land. I put the still struggling chick down gently and watched it scamper off into the colony.

About a month after our arrival at St Andrew's Bay a few adult king penguins started to walk up from the beach to visit our hut. At the end of our seven months' stay, it was a regular daily occurrence. Although the distance from the beach to the hut was only four hundred yards, it would take the kings a good hour to reach us. This was due to their short legs and tiny steps, and because they constantly tripped over loose stones and stopped every now and then for a breather. They viewed the hut with great curiosity, circling it three or four times, inspecting all the objects around the hut such as the sledge, snow shoes, fuel drums and the washing line. One afternoon, when we were at the hut and twenty or thirty kings came to visit us, they circled the hut two or three times, nibbling and pecking at every object and then moved off towards the washing line. This had guy ropes spread-eagled out supporting the poles. The penguins got the ropes round their ankles so that when they tried to move away they only succeeded in tripping themselves up. One king got the rope caught between its legs, but instead of stepping out over it, it tried to walk up it until the guy rope actually lifted the king off its feet. The king was furious and attacked the rope with its flippers and beak, then lost its balance and fell off.

After a while, the kings started to try to climb up onto the wooden platform outside the door of the hut. However, the step up from the ground to the platform was a bit too high for short penguin legs, so we built a ramp for them out of flat stones lying around nearby. It didn't take the kings long to try out the ramp and get up onto the platform and stand right by the open door and stare into the hut at us. Sometimes they would lean back on their heels in the resting position, watching us at work in the hut and I am sure that, if they could, they would have folded their flippers in front of them as we do our arms!

By January, the colony was in full swing. The majority of year-old chicks had moulted and moved away from the colony to stand in groups along the shore, having been pushed out by the breeding adults. There were late-moulting kings all round the colony and up on the surrounding glaciers, and thousands of kings in the colony were going through their courtship mating and egg-laying and the first few chicks were even on the point of hatching. They were all up to something, even the pathetic, starving chicks left to die along the beach. Their parents had deserted them, so the chicks were no longer being fed. It was now too late in the season for the adults to continue to feed their year-old chicks and to fit in another breeding season. So they would abandon the late-developing chicks and go to sea to fatten up before returning to moult.

By mid-February, the main colony was already full with the early breeders and the late-comers had to nest wherever they could. Some nested down towards the beach, and others, much to our amazement, chose the old bed of the Cook Glacier melt stream. We didn't think this at all wise, because a few days of warm weather would flood the melt stream and destroy the eggs. But we decided that the kings probably knew what they were doing and it turned out that they did. The melt stream never flooded.

One day in April, we noticed a disturbance in the sea just by the Rocky Point, where the penguins launched themselves into the sea. The kings on the rocks had quickly backed away from the water's edge and were watching a lot of splashing and foaming water just a few yards out at sea. The splashing suddenly stopped and the sea became calm again and we wondered what on earth it was all about. Then a leopard seal broke surface with a king, still very much alive, in its mouth. Annie and I tore down the tussock cliff with all the cameras, but it was all over.

Leopard seals prefer very cold water and during the summer they usually retreat south of the island. By April, however, temperatures have begun to drop and as winter draws near, the water of St Andrew's Bay fills with bits of ice and is cold enough to attract them back again.

We spent hours out on that Rocky Point with the penguins waiting for the leopard seal to strike again. We nearly froze to death with no shelter from the winds that roared down off the mountains and glaciers, or from the spray of the surf that crashed round the rocks. I was forever having to wipe the lenses clean and, in the evenings, the whole camera had to be cleaned to get rid of the salt. But it was worth it. We filmed five separate leopard seal kills, all from different angles. Compared to the sea-lion catching and killing a gentoo penguin in the Falklands, the leopard seal kills were rather dull. It simply hid in the seaweed just a few yards from Rocky Point, occasionally sticking its nose up out of the water to take in a breath of air, and patiently waited for a king to swim within striking range. There was no exciting chase or battle. The seal simply grabbed the unfortunate penguin and with its horrendously long and needle-sharp teeth, bit deep into the poor bird.

That first bite rarely killed the penguin outright. Sometimes the seal would submerge and stay under for a good minute or more with the penguin still firmly in its mouth. Seals can stay underwater much longer than penguins, so that by the time the two re-emerged, the king was half drowned. The seal would dive repeatedly until the penguin died, then it would thrash the king violently from side to side, ripping the bird apart and eating it. Giant petrels, gulls and Cape pigeons would pour in from all directions, attracted by the thrashing on the surface and, bobbing up and down on the rough sea, they would grab any tiny scraps floating about, careful not to get too close to the leopard seal.

At other times, the seal was more cruel and would tear off a flipper or maybe a leg. While the seal ate whatever it had managed to tear off, the king, still alive, would make desperate efforts to reach the safety of the rocks. If its flipper had been torn off, it could only swim round and round in circles. If a leg or part of the body had been torn away, the bird would be too weak from loss of blood, and in such a severe state of shock, its efforts to get away would be far too slow and the seal would grab it and drag it further out to sea. After a few mintues, nothing remained but a slight reddish tinge in the sea.

9

THE LONGEST TREK

December 21st was mid-summer's day – the longest day – down in our part of the world and at 11.30 p.m. we photographed each other standing by the hut with the snow-covered mountains and glaciers in the background. There was no need for any flash equipment. The snow had all gone from the low-lying land and hills, and although it snowed several days a month, it never settled for long. The wind continued to howl down from the mountains and glaciers with a bitterness that made us huddle behind the few big boulders near the king penguin colony while out filming. The wind was so cold some days that it penetrated through all our layers of clothing and after several hours of being out, we had to return to the hut for something hot to drink, to warm us up again. During warm spells, the melt streams from the glaciers roared down and out to sea but we would always try to cross the streams as it meant a much shorter walk to the penguin colony. Often, however, we would end up with bootfuls of ice-cold water. We would then spend the whole day filming with cold, wet feet. We soon learnt that if we could see the Heaney melt stream from the hut it was too deep for us to cross and we would have to walk the extra mile or two upstream and over the snout of the glacier. If we couldn't see the melt stream from the hut we knew it was crossable. It really depended on the temperature. Warm, and the melt stream rose, cold, and the stream slowed down. But whether the stream was crossable or not, the current was always very swift. We found that the more things we carried on our backs, the easier it was for us to cross as the extra weight helped us keep our feet firmly on the ground. We would hold on to each other while crossing, each one helping the other to keep her balance.

One of the mechanics who helped to dismantle the crashed helicopter did not realise just how swift the current was and tried to wade across the melt stream. Within a couple of seconds, he was swept two hundred yards down the stream where he managed to struggle to one of the banks. At one point, Annie and I also got swept off our feet when trying to cross the Heaney melt stream. Luckily we had no camera equipment with us. Hanging onto each other for support, we soon realised the stream was too deep and the current too swift for us to get across. It was while we were attempting to turn back that the raging current knocked Annie's feet from under her and so she grabbed me for extra support, causing me to lose my balance. We both went under, splashing and struggling in our heavy clothing. Later, apart from the discomfort of the ice-cold ducking, we had a good laugh about it all as water poured out of the pockets of our anoraks and from inside our boots. From then on, we were more careful.

As the summer wore on, the little stream that ran by our hut and provided us with fresh drinking water grew smaller and smaller. After a while it was impossible to collect water with a saucepan, so I dug a deep hole in the stream bed which filled up, allowing me to get the saucepan in. But that was not our only problem. The elephant seals were a permanent headache when it came to our drinking water. Hundreds of young weaned pups, shedding immature bulls and females would come up the stream from the beach to wallow in the water, turning it into a thick, muddy mess. There was nothing we could do except fight off the seals, which we did with our ski-sticks every morning for several weeks, gently prodding them or tapping their noses until they finally got the message and rarely came near the hut or the pool of water. By January, the little stream completely dried up and we had to walk some way towards the Heaney Glacier where there was a lovely stream that came down from the hills above. If only that stream had been a little nearer! The walk back to the hut with full containers was a bit of a slog.

On Christmas Eve, we unpacked the crate of food and presents which *Endurance* had left with us and dutifully hid everything away from each other except the Christmas stockings which my mother had sent. These we hung up at the end of our bunks. On Christmas Day 1981 it snowed nearly all day. When we had got through all our usual chores, I looked out of the window and decided that it wasn't going to be a working day. Not far from the hut, a herd of reindeer were quietly grazing. They had now become quite used to us and some days would swim across the melt streams in search of food. Although the day was bright we lit the Tilley lamp to give us some extra warmth. I felt that Christmas Day warranted this wild extravagance. In no time at all, the hut was comparatively warm and cosy and we sat down to unpack our stockings. They were full of useful things like underpants and toothpaste and in among the wrapping paper we found a marvellous note from my father saying he couldn't remember which stocking was which, even though my mother had gone to great pains to explain to him. However, he said that he didn't think we would have much trouble sorting them out as he gathered the knicker sizes were vastly different. He was quite right.

Nick Barker had sent us a bottle of champagne and Jim Parker, the ex-Governor of the Falkland Islands who, together with his wife, was now back in England, had sent a jigsaw. Other friends in the Falklands had sent sherry, mince pies and chocolates and both Annie's mother and mine had sent an enormous food parcel. We went through these to pick out some tinned ham and pâté for our lunch. We toasted our families then thought about our Christmas dinner. There seemed to be no end to the goodies we could choose from. In the end, we settled for chicken chunks in white wine sauce, tinned asparagus in Hollandaise sauce and tinned potatoes, accompanied by a bottle of white wine and some port. After that, we got out the washing board – our table was too small – and set about doing the jigsaw which we found was much easier to do after we'd had a few sips of the delicious sloe gin Annie's mother had sent. We went to bed that night glowing contentedly.

During the last few days of 1981 we had a humdinger of a gale. Early in the morning, it was fairly calm with perhaps twenty knots of wind, which was quite usual. As it was sunny, we decided to do some washing – pyjamas, sleeping bag liners and pillow cases. By the time we had finished and were hanging everything up to dry, the wind had increased to about sixty knots. I was a little worried that everything was going to be torn to shreds, but, as it happened, everything was dry in twenty minutes – the quickest drying session we ever had.

We decided to go and do some filming of the gale but the wind was throwing so much sand about that we could hardly see where we were going. It got into our eyes and ears, down our necks and even into our mouths. Our faces were left stinging from the impact and, of course, the cameras and lenses were covered by it. At some points, where the wind roared down and round the corners of the cliffs, we could barely stand and were often forced backwards. Such gales left us exhausted and on New Year's Eve 1981 we were so tired that we couldn't keep awake until midnight and woke up next day to a miserable New Year's Day of rain and snow.

In mid-January, we decided to walk to Royal Bay, about seven miles south, but ten miles on foot. There was a small wooden hut there which BAS kindly allowed us to use. There were several things in the area I wanted to film, such as the huge Ross Glacier which is seventy feet high where it meets the sea. Also, I wanted to record macaroni penguins and blue-eyed shags, none of which we had at St Andrew's Bay. We had a rucksack each full of cameras, lenses, film, batteries and film magazines plus the tape recorder and microphone and the tripod. We were horrified when we worked out that each rucksack weighed forty-five pounds.

The first hour took us to the south end of St Andrew's Bay and the second hour found us in Doris Bay. There we had a rest and collected two large whalebones and a marvellous pair of reindeer antlers, to be brought back to our hut later on. For the next four hours it was all up hill and the heavy loads on our backs seemed to grow heavier and heavier. Our rests got more and more frequent and our legs and backs began to ache like hell. If only we had had lighter loads I think we would have thoroughly enjoyed the walk, but we were bent right over slogging upwards, forcing one foot in front of the other as we climbed up the valley of Doris Bay until we reached the foot of the Nachtigal Glacier. There we found a lovely little waterfall and we stopped to rest and have a drink and a wash. We looked up at the glacier to the snow-covered mountains and beyond and sighed, knowing that we had to go up there with our heavy burdens. We had to climb up onto the right-hand side of the glacier where stones and rubble lay, as we did not have any crampons to climb up on the ice. It was absolute murder as the rubble lay on the ice only an inch or so deep and we were constantly slipping and sliding as the stones shot from under our feet. Although the air was cold from the glacier we poured with sweat and grunted and groaned as we heaved our heavy loads higher and higher.

Half-way up the glacier on the other side, we could see a deep gully which we hoped was the route to Royal Bay. We had some contour maps which we referred to constantly but because these were somewhat basic there were times when we were not absolutely sure what point we had reached. We started to cross over, walking very carefully so as not to fall on the hard ice and watching out for cracks and holes that covered the surface. We were a little nervous as we peered down some of the holes and could hear the mass of running water underneath the ice we were standing on. Small cracks we jumped over, large ones we had to find a way round. When we got to the other side, we sat down, tired and hungry, on some rocks and had another rest. We had with us several bars of chocolate and a few boiled sweets. We continued on for a little longer and, at last, reached the highest point and started going down the gully. The centre of the gully was filled with snow and ice, a small ice-field and we almost ran down this digging our heels in hard to stop us getting out of control. We were nearly beyond caring whether there was firm ground under the snow or not. At the bottom of the ice-field, we came to perhaps the worst part of the whole trip.

The ice was thin and far too dangerous to walk on. This meant we had to edge our way down the side, clinging to the side of the gorge which rose above us in a sheer vertical wall impossible to grasp. Underfoot, the melted ice had uncovered the scree which was mostly loose bits of slate which shot out alarmingly under us with every step we took. I went first, concentrating on one move at a time. Behind me, though I didn't dare look, I could hear the roar of the water. One slip, I knew, and I would fall backwards onto the ice which was sure to crack under the impact of the heavily laden rucksack. Even if, by some miracle, that *didn't* happen, I would almost certainly meet instant death as a slide down the ice would send me crashing against the cliff edge. With my face pressed against the face of the gorge, I felt for another foothold, desperately trying to grasp at a protruding rock that always seemed to be beyond my reach. If I were going to survive this, I realised I needed to use all my powers of concentration. Pausing for a moment, I glanced back along the wall of the gorge and saw, to my horror, that Annie had become frozen with fear. Mesmerised by the awfulness of our situation, she was clinging to the wall, unable to move in either direction.

'Come on, *do* it,' I shouted. 'Move your hand up to the right.' Her eyes were closed and she gave no sign of hearing me.

'Move,' I yelled. Perhaps the noise of the torrent was drowning my voice. We were both exhausted after our long trek and I was starting to get cramp. I longed to be back in the safety and comfort of the hut at St Andrew's Bay. Annie opened her eyes and shook her head.

'I can't move,' she gasped. 'If I do, my rucksack will topple me backwards.'

Our rucksacks were far too heavy and, loaded as they were with the tripod and ski-sticks, they were constantly unbalancing us. On the other hand, we couldn't stay there for ever. We *had* to go forward.

'Come on, Annie, we'll move one step at a time. We've got to get across.' We had only three hundred feet to cover, but the nightmare seemed unending and it took us over an hour to cover that short distance. When we reached the end, Annie produced a miniature of brandy and though I hate the smell, I took a gulp and felt the comforting warmth sink into my body. The ordeal we had just been through had made us sweat a lot and I looked round for some water to drink. The water that comes out from under the glacier is usually cloudy as it has picked up bits of dirt and stones from the ground, and the only water you can safely drink straightaway is surface water. So thirsty was Annie that she was already down on her hands and knees with her face in a minute pool drinking from its clear, fresh water.

By the time we got to the bottom of the gully, we found ourselves in Whale Valley which leads into Royal Bay, a long narrow valley. At last we could see the sea, although it was still a long way off. We had been walking for seven hours by this time and the only thing that kept us going was the thought of having to spend the night out. We had another rest but the depressing fact was that when we returned our rucksacks wouldn't be any lighter, except perhaps for our toothpaste tubes!

We made the mistake of walking down the centre of the valley where a river flowed and where the ground was very soft and spongy which was very tiring on the legs. They were virtually on the point of collapse by this time. We should have climbed up onto firmer ground but neither of us had the energy to do so. Bent over with our heavy loads, on and on we plodded, our eyes fixed to the ground. The valley seemed to go on for ever until, finally, we could see two small gentoo penguin colonies and then I knew for certain that we were about to enter Moltke Harbour, part of Royal Bay. At the bottom of the valley, we turned left round a hill and there, at last, was the BAS hut.

Near the hut were several large tents belonging to the Joint Services Expedition which had come out on *Endurance* just before Christmas, as this was their base camp. Two of the men were at the camp: Lt-Commander Hamish Craig of the Royal Navy and Bombardier Dick Aderton of the 7/45 Commando Group. Heaven knows what we would have done without them. Having dumped our loads by the hut, we went into one of the tents and collapsed onto some packing cases and they filled us with hot, sweet tea and a huge steaming stew. Hamish was doing some scientific work on the reindeer and Dick was the radio man. One would have expected us to sleep like the dead that night, but we were so stiff all over that neither of us slept very well and we felt pretty ghastly the next morning.

Our intention was to walk over to Calf Head to film the macaroni penguins, a short walk of only three hours, the men said, and easy going. It would help to loosen up the stiff legs and backs! They both wanted to go there themselves and they would help to carry some of our loads. We didn't leave the camp until midday as it poured with rain but, finally, we set off for what we thought was going to be a jolly little walk. No such luck! Perhaps it was because we were tired, stiff and sore before we even started, but every hill was agony. Dick was the climber and led the way, stopping and resting until we caught up with him. We moaned and groaned as we traversed up the steep, loose scree slopes and Dick said 'Not far now' and 'Just over the next ridge', to encourage us. We made it to Calf Head in good time, considering we stopped on some of the high ridges to film the scenes below and the beautiful crystal-clear lakes formed by the melt streams that flowed from glaciers and snow-fields. It wasn't until we dropped down off the mountains onto the finger of land called Calf Head that we hit grass and a bit of greenery.

Then we had another climb ahead of us up a steep tussock hill and down the other side to reach the penguin colony. At last, there they were, thousands of them, nesting in the tussock grass and on open rocky patches, all with chicks a few weeks old. The macaroni penguins are very like the rockhoppers both in habit and looks. About twenty inches high with long, yellow head feathers, they pop out of the sea and land on gently sloping rocks and climb several hundred feet up the cliffs, over well-worn routes to reach their colony. They don't make real nests, just a few stones and bits of tussock grass and they lay two white eggs in November. They were extremely aggressive towards us as we worked our way through the tussock grass to reach one of the open areas to film them. We were attacked from all sides, sharp beaks stabbing at our legs and flippers bashing us as we went by. We were forced to use our feet to push them aside to let us pass. They not only attacked us but each other, forever fighting and screaming amongst themselves, guarding their two little chicks and their tiny territories. By five p.m., we had finished filming in the colony, but I still hadn't got all I wanted. I had noticed a small giant petrel colony that I wanted to film. We had slogged so long and so hard to get here, I was determined not to leave until I had filmed that as well, so we decided to stay the night, despite the fact that we hadn't got our sleeping bags, toothbrushes or hairbrushes with us. However, the two men did have a tent with them, as they came over to Calf Head every week to do some scientific work and they also had a small supply of food, fuel and a paraffin burner. So we climbed back up the steep tussock hill and down the other side to a flat, grassy area where their supplies were kept, and pitched the tent and brewed up a hot meal.

Because we had not planned to stay, we were not really prepared for

153

the night ahead of us. Although the tent was a two-man tent, we all piled in and huddled together to keep warm. We had emergency bivvy bags which were supposed to give us some protection by reflecting our own body heat but the warm air condensed inside the bags and left us in a very damp condition. Dick had persuaded us to take off our boots and put our padded gloves on our feet instead – we could warm our hands by keeping them between our legs. Then we all managed somehow or other to stretch out top to tail which, as the night wore on, turned out to be disastrous as it meant that every time I moved I got Dick's gloved foot in my face. And in case there was any remote chance that we might drop off to sleep, Hamish punctuated the night with his snores which we named the Red Arrow fly past. Poor Hamish. The final torture was being kept awake by the stones which dug into our backs.

We crawled out of the tent at about six a.m., cold, damp and miserable. For a while a thick sea fog swirled around our heads until the sun got strong enough to burn it all away. At last, we began to dry out and warm up. Back at the macaroni penguin colony, we filmed them coming ashore and climbing up their well-used paths to their colony. While we were filming them coming ashore we saw a young white fur seal sleeping on the rocks – not an albino, as it had dark eyes, but it was certainly the palest fur seal I have ever seen. We also saw and filmed an adult bull fur seal chasing a macaroni penguin over the rocks and into the sea. The seal caught the penguin, thrashed it on the surface of the water a few times and then let it go and the penguin, unharmed but rather shaken, hopped ashore. It had turned into a lovely day, and while we filmed and photographed the penguins and giant petrels Dick and Hamish went to sleep in the sun.

We finished all the filming by mid-afternoon and after a short rest to allow the sun to go down a little, we set off back to Royal Bay, up and down the slippery mountains, reaching camp as it began to grow dark. After a huge supper we slept like logs. Our last day at Royal Bay was lovely, the sun shone and we didn't go far in any direction. We filmed the huge Ross Glacier with its seventy-foot ice cliff which stops at the sea. The glacier was calving – bits breaking off and falling into the sea – and we could hear constant bangs and cracks like rifle shots as the huge chunks of ice crashed into the sea. We found a small blue-eyed shag colony under some cliffs and a Weddell seal lying on the rocks. The whole afternoon was spent trying to stalk some reindeer to film them, but we were not very successful. I would have liked to have spent a few more days at Royal Bay, but I was eager to get back to St Andrew's Bay as

I was expecting the first king penguin eggs to hatch in a few days' time. We packed up all our equipment and started the long, hard slog back. This time, though, it was much more pleasant.

Dick and Hamish decided to come back with us to have a look round St Andrew's Bay and have a change of scenery. We were delighted as it meant that they could carry half our loads. They didn't have to bring anything with them as we had tents and extra sleeping bags at our hut. This time we avoided the glaciers by taking a more direct route with a higher and harder climb but with different scenery for me to film. We went straight up Whale Valley and then climbed the steep sides of Mount Krokisius. From the top, we could see Royal Bay, Doris Bay and St Andrew's Bay stretching out in the distance. Down on the beach at Doris Bay, we came to a grinding halt. The melt stream that runs out of the Nachtigal Glacier was in full flood after several days of warm weather. Repeatedly, we tried to cross it at different places, but each time we were forced back by the depth and the very swift current. We got absolutely soaked and frozen by the ice-cold water. The thought of having to walk all the way up the valley to reach the glacier, cross over it and then walk all the way down the valley again didn't appeal to us. A stretch of water, no more than forty feet wide, was all that was stopping us.

With each attempt to find a place, the crossing became more dangerous. Standing in freezing water up to our thighs, our legs became numb so that we were unable to feel the ground or indeed to know if there was any ground there at all. Missing our step in the water was a constant danger. Finally, after an hour, we made it but by now it was getting dark and our feet and legs were frozen. We stripped off our boots, socks and trousers, wrung them out and then started on our way again. The last lap, fortunately, was easy. We had to walk along from Doris Bay to St Andrew's Bay and then over the snouts of the Cook and Heaney Glacier and back to the hut.

The men stayed with us for three days, having a look at the wildlife. We had a great time and enjoyed their company, although our hut was too small for four people to sit around and eat and we were forever tripping over each other. In the evenings, we would all huddle together in the hut with the Tilley lamp going, telling each other stories, me about Africa and Dick about Norway, where he goes every year to do his Arctic training with the commandos. We were sad to see them go, little guessing that we would soon be sharing the hut with three other men and for much longer!

On 27 January we tuned in to the radio to hear, to our surprise, a

155

sturdy male-voice choir singing happy birthday to Annie! It was, indeed, Annie's birthday and the men from BAS at Bird Island had heard a birthday telex coming over the radio to Annie from her mother. Those beautiful deep voices gave us quite a thrill. We were sure we could detect a Welsh voice among the six of them. It had been one of those near-perfect days at St Andrew's Bay. After the Bird Island serenade, we sat down to a celebration dinner of tinned ham and asparagus, finished off with a bottle of wine which we had saved for the occasion.

10

DROPPING IN
FOR TEA

Our next walk was to Grytviken about ten miles to the north. Having learnt from our trip to Royal Bay, we tried to cut down on weight. Instead of taking a tube of toothpaste each, we took only one between us. This time, I took a smaller and lighter camera, my Bolex, and only a few small lenses. However, we had to take quite a few extra things with us like sleeping bags and a change of clothing for when we got to Grytviken. We didn't need the recording machine this time but, even so, our rucksacks still weighed between thirty and forty pounds. Again there was nothing we could do. We needed it all.

We planned to walk first to Cumberland Bay and when we told the BAS team this they offered to come across the Bay by boat from Grytviken and pick us up.

We had decided to go to Grytviken as there were a number of things I wanted to photograph. When we'd previously landed there, on our way to St Andrew's Bay, I'd paid a brief visit to the whaling station but I hadn't had time to take any photographs, nor had there been an opportunity to film the BAS team at work – another thing I wanted to do. Mount Paget, the highest peak in South Georgia, was clearly visible, on a clear day, from Grytviken, and I hoped to get some good shots of it while I was over there. But perhaps most exciting of all was the opportunity to photograph the island's largest glacier – Nordenskjold – which lay at the end of our route to Cumberland Bay.

So, on 10 February, we left our hut on what looked like a promising day. The sun was shining with just a few white fluffy clouds lazily sailing by. The first hour and a half was the worst part of the trip. From the hut, we had to climb up a very steep loose scree slope twelve hundred feet high. With the sun shining and little wind to cool us, it was very hot work. Neither of us was interested in breaking records, so the fact that we stopped every few hundred yards to cool down and catch our breath on our way up was not unusual. One part was rather unpleasant when we had to walk across some very loose scree and every foothold had to be checked to make sure that it would take our weight. One bad slip on the loose rocks and we would have shot down the slope for several hundred feet. The panoramic view of St Andrew's Bay from the top was beautiful: snow-covered mountains, the three glaciers, the melt streams and the penguin colony. I managed to get some film of it just before a huge bank of cloud formed overhead.

We scrambled over the little pass that leads down into Luisa Bay and gazed on new land before us. Luisa Bay is small and narrow, littered with dangerous-looking rocks all along the coastline. The valley leading up to the mountains is completely barren, not a blade of grass in sight, just a mass of moraine and scree slopes. While we looked at Luisa Bay the clouds thickened and began to threaten us with a little rain, so I decided that we ought to press on to our destination before we got too wet. Down we went into the valley, passing a freshwater lake fed by several small streams, and up on the other side we struggled to reach our next pass. We stopped by one of the many crystal-clear streams to have a drink, a bar of chocolate and a rest. The relief of getting those heavy rucksacks off our backs, even for five minutes, was indescribable.

The view from the next pass was of Hound Bay, where we would be spending the night. BAS had a small field hut tucked behind a hill right down on the beach which we had to find. The difference between Luisa Bay and Hound Bay was very striking. Luisa Bay was barren and desolate, with little colour to cheer the place up, whereas Hound Bay was very green with a coarse type of grass growing five hundred feet up the hillside. The bay was very long and narrow, ending in a grey sandy beach. Behind the beach, stretching for several miles, was the green Lonnberg Valley that finally met up with the huge Nordenskjold Glacier. A melt stream from the glacier wound its way down the valley, cutting through the beach and out into the sea. From the top of the pass, we had an easy walk down a long gentle slope that went all the way down to the coast. Walking on the tough tufted grass wasn't much fun: conditions were ideal for twisting ankles. It had also got rather wet and boggy underfoot and our climbing boots were soon saturated, so that our feet made horrible squelching noises. We ran down the last hundred feet into the tussock grass and while we weaved our way in and out of it, we found several giant petrel nests, all with very large chicks on them. I

158

ABOVE The king penguin colony at St Andrew's Bay

LEFT A leopard seal showing its razor-sharp teeth (*Peter Stark*, BAS)

FOLLOWING PAGES A dawn shot taken on the beach at St Andrew's Bay

Emptying my boots after a wet crossing through a melt stream

OPPOSITE PAGE
ABOVE LEFT   Outside the hut on Christmas Day 1981. Our Christmas stockings and the
boxes of food had been delivered to us by HMS *Endurance* a week before
ABOVE RIGHT   My parents in their flying suits arriving at St Andrew's Bay
BELOW   The Heaney Glacier melt stream breaking through the sandy beach wall
OVERLEAF   Walking up the Heaney Glacier

ABOVE With
Hamish Craig and
Dick Aderton *(R)*
from the Joint
Services Expedition
at the top of Whale
Valley on our way
back from Royal Bay

RIGHT Resting on
one of our walks out
of St Andrew's Bay

PREVIOUS PAGE
Filming on the
Heaney Glacier

ABOVE Blue-eyed shags on an ice floe that had just broken off one of the many glaciers on South Georgia

LEFT A macaroni penguin sheltering its chick

FOLLOWING PAGES The Nordenskjold Glacier, the largest on South Georgia. The snout of the glacier is over two miles wide and a hundred feet high

OPPOSITE ABOVE
A Wasp helicopter
landing on the flight
deck of HMS
Endurance at dawn
during our rescue

OPPOSITE BELOW   The
Argentinian
submarine *Santa Fe*
grounded and tied
up to the jetty of the
old whaling station
at Grytviken

RIGHT   Some of the
Royal Marines at
Grytviken after the
retaking of South
Georgia

BELOW   Leaving
South Georgia on
HMS *Antrim* with a
final glimpse of
HMS *Endurance* at
Grytviken

LEFT With the twelve BAS personnel on board HMS *Antelope*, a few days before reaching Ascension Island

BELOW LEFT On the fore deck of HMS *Antelope*, which was later sunk

BELOW RIGHT Facing the media on arrival at Brize Norton, 2.35 a.m., 14 May 1982 *(Royal Navy photograph)*

made a mental note that I must film them – but not now. It was just on the point of raining and we had to find the BAS hut quickly.

Once down on the stony shore, we turned left towards the head of the bay and after a few hundred yards found the green painted wooden hut tucked behind a hill. We groaned with relief and helped each other off with our rucksacks, sitting on the doorstep of the hut and rubbing our shoulders back to life. It had taken us four hours to cover the six miles between Hound Bay and St Andrew's Bay. The hut was larger than the one at St Andrew's Bay but divided into two instead of three. The first section was the cloakroom and kitchen combined and the other part was the living and sleeping area with two wooden bunks. The hut was in poor shape, with the green paint on the outside flaking off. Later, when it rained, we had several bad leaks through the roof and the walls, but it was home for the next few hours.

Having unpacked, we rummaged through the food supply at the hut and found everything that we needed plus several empty rusty tins and a few half-eaten tins of jam, butter and cheese with mould growing on the top, which we buried. After hot soup and ration biscuits, we went out to see what Hound Bay had to offer. Sharing the tussock grass with the nesting giant petrels were many elephant seals snoring away and shedding their skins.

It was at Hound Bay that we found two new species of birds to add to our list. We found a solitary chinstrap penguin on the beach and, ten feet outside the hut, we sat and listened to a South Georgia pipit singing to us. The pipit was the more surprising of the two, as we had been told many times by BAS that they only lived on the off-lying islands where there were no rats to prey on them. The pipit is a very small bird with a streaked brown body, white tail feathers and a slender bill, very similar to the meadow pipit at home. It sang its little song to us for a few minutes and then flew off. After supper, we walked along the shore until we came to a fresh-water stream. The water was icy and it was raining, but we scrubbed out all the pots and pans and then, putting on our bath hats, had a wash ourselves and that night we slept like logs.

The weather didn't look very good when we left Hound Bay next morning to cover the last four miles to the Sorling Valley hut. The clouds were very low and it looked as though it was going to rain again. The pass we had to climb over was just below the cloud line, so we decided to give it a go. The first obstacle was the melt stream that cut through the beach. Not wanting to get soaking feet, we stripped off our boots, socks and trousers and waded through the water. We then ran around the beach for a few minutes with our shirt-tails flapping, to get some feeling back into our legs and feet. At the end of the beach, we started to climb up to the pass to Sorling Valley. The first few hundred feet were slow going as we struggled over thick tufts of grass. Up on the moraine our pace quickened. Our map showed us that we had to pass one large lake at the top of the pass on our left. We were a little surprised when we found six lakes all widely scattered, so we passed the whole lot on our left. While we were walking beside the lakes, it began to snow, lightly at first and then gradually heavier. We were right at the top of the pass, our highest point, about eight hundred feet, with the visibility still reasonable, so we kept going. We were wet, cold and miserable, our jackets sodden and our rucksacks were beginning to let in the wet snow.

We reached the southern end of Cumberland Bay but our journey was not yet over as we still hadn't found the hut. In fact, we weren't really sure where exactly it was. The snow was beginning to settle on the ground and visibility had dropped right down to fifty feet so that every few minutes we had to stop to check our map, getting even colder and more miserable as the journey dragged on. And then, suddenly, round a bend, we came upon it.

We quickly found two Tilley lamps and got them going and stripped off our wet clothes, hanging them up all over the hut on bits of string. Dressed only in our thermal underwear, we climbed into our damp sleeping bags. The hut was smaller than the one at Hound Bay, with a tiny porch and the main living/sleeping and cooking area in one. After an hour or so the little hut began to warm up and we emerged from our sleeping bags. We stayed in the hut, had some lunch and sorted out all the food boxes, burning any rubbish we found. The BAS team had been over the previous day and left a radio for us so that we were able to call them up to say that we had finally arrived.

Before going to bed that night, we went outside to have a wash and had there been anyone remotely near to see, we must have looked an odd sight – two young women in thermal underwear, climbing boots and bath hats, cleaning their teeth in a snow storm.

Next morning the BAS team at Grytviken sent a boat across the bay to collect us. At the very end of the bay we could see the two-mile-wide cascade of the Nordenskjold Glacier stopped dead in its tracks by the sea, its ice-cliffs towering a hundred feet above the water's edge. In order to get as close as possible for filming, we transferred to a rubber dinghy which allowed us to manoeuvre close to the glacier. Blocks of ice littered the bay from the constant calving of the glacier. In fact, as we passed along the huge towering ice-cliff a huge piece of ice, about the size of a house, broke off from the front of the glacier and crashed into the sea with a tremendous splash, causing several large waves. Blues, greens and dazzling white shone out from the solid ice floes. Cormorants rested on these floating blocks of ice while they were out fishing.

We were allowed to land by the side of the Nordenskjold and climb up one side of it so that I could film looking down the whole length of the glacier snout. The glacier was very heavily crevassed with huge holes and cracks and, in places, was very ragged where bits had fallen off. Every now and then we heard sharp cracks as another piece of ice broke away and fell into the sea. The glacier groaned and creaked as millions of tons of ice came under pressure and shifted slightly.

I could have gone on filming the glacier for hours but I only had a certain amount of footage set aside for it, so once I had got all I needed, we re-boarded the launch and headed for Grytviken.

There were twenty-eight men at the BAS camp when we visited it and the Deputy Base Commander, Steve Martin, kindly gave up his bedroom for us so that we were living in the lap of luxury – sleeping in beds with sheets and pillows. We had a hot steaming bath every night and the final delight was to wash our clothes in a washing machine. The dining-room was enormous. The table was made of pine with room for thirty people and the food that went on it was delicious. The first evening, after a bath, a change of clothes and a huge dinner, we sat down in comfortable armchairs, sipping port and watching a film. This, indeed, was the life!

We spent four days in Grytviken. Once the men had got used to us and we to them, we had a marvellous time. Everyone relaxed and generally accepted us as part of the household. They were always asking if there was anything they could do for us, or get us, and, of course, they wanted to know how the filming was going. We needed a few small items to take back with us to St Andrew's Bay which were found and stored for our return. Annie disappeared for hours with the cook down in the storeroom. If she had had her way, she would have tried to take back to our hut a rucksack of goodies, but I knew we were already carrying our maximum weight, so very reluctantly, she only accepted some fresh garlic and a tin of ham.

When we had sorted out our various bits and pieces, the Base Commander Pete Witty very kindly showed us round the place. We went through all the buildings on the base and saw the machine shops, radio shack, met. office and diving equipment store. Shackleton House, the living quarters of the twenty-eight men was due to be closed down at the end of the season and the number of men reduced to eight for the winter. It was considered uneconomic to keep Shackleton House running for eight men, so Colman House, an existing building, was being gutted and rebuilt. BAS could no longer afford to keep a large number of men at Grytviken, and reducing the numbers by a third was part of the cut-backs. No one seemed to know what would happen to Shackleton House, whether it would be left to rot or whether it would be pulled down and the materials used for something else. I was glad that I was able to live in Shackleton House during its last few months.

Later, Pete took us to the old whaling station, a mile away from the base. Both Annie and I had visited it during our first visit way back in October, but we had been on our own and didn't really know the history of the place or what everything was. This second visit with someone who was able to show us round made all the difference. Up to eight hundred men had lived at Grytviken whaling station for two years or more at a stretch. We wandered through their old dormitories, dining-rooms, recreation rooms and the little chapel. I could almost hear the tough weather-beaten men plodding about, playing and laughing. They had worked very hard, twelve hours on, twelve hours off in appalling conditions. The only highlight of the day was meal time, when they had as much food as they wanted. We visited the vast machine and store sheds where thousands of pounds worth of equipment was lying about all over the floor, smashed, broken and uncared for. Pete explained that for the last five years, various ships had been visiting Grytviken to obtain fresh water and to have a day or two of rest. The huge crews on board would visit the old whaling station and have the time of their lives smashing every conceivable thing they could get their hands on. Polish and Russian trawlers were the worst offenders. Old records were found torn up and scattered all over the floor. There was also a lot of brand-new machinery left lying around – tools, bolts and spares all carefully greased and packed away. The whaling trade had virtually ceased by the 1960s but Grytviken and Leith had been sub-leased briefly to some Japanese companies. The whalers, expecting to return, had left everything ready for the next season but the venture had proved unsuccessful and they had never come back.

Pete told us how the whale was winched out of the sea and hauled up on to a ramp leading to the shed. There, the men stood on each side of the whale with their knives ready to begin flensing the animal. Flensing knives are sharp curved blades attached to long poles, and sometimes the men had to climb up on to the back of the whale and work from there. When the whale had been flensed, the blubber, meat and bone were separated. Each part was cooked for hours until all the valuable oil had been extracted and stored in huge tanks. The bones were crushed into a fine powder and sent back to England to be used as fertiliser. The meat was also ground down and dried, to be used as stock feed. Somehow, it was horrifyingly easy to imagine the grinding of the winches, the men yelling and the giant cookers hissing and steaming and above it all the overpowering, sick smell of the whale oil.

On the Monday, when everyone had returned to normal, we went round the base filming various people at work. The radio operator, in his little room surrounded by a mass of impressive equipment, spends all day talking to the other British Antarctic bases like Halley Bay, Rothera, Faraday and Signy Island, finding out if all is well and collecting weather reports. He would also talk to various fishing vessels working in the Antarctic, taking their weather observations and ice conditions, gathering them all together and sending it all on to Buenos Aires. Telexes and telegrams came through twice daily from Port Stanley and any traffic would be sent back there. He would also call up *Endurance*, and the two BAS ships, the *John Biscoe* and the *Bransfield*. Positions would be given together with weather and ice reports.

Weather observations were also taken at Grytviken. The BAS launch, *Albatross*, would go out nearly every day, weather permitting, to allow divers to dive down deep into the icy sea to collect rare specimens of one sort or another, or to take other scientists trawling to catch fish or krill for further studies. In Shackleton House, we found scientists engrossed over their microscopes, peering at strange little creatures in a tube. One scientist showed us a strange, tiny beetle which under artificial conditions had its body temperature reduced to a very low degree when it ceased all movement and appeared to be dead. Then suddenly, as the temperature was raised again it sprang back to life.

We had a wonderful time at Grytviken and were spoilt terribly by all the men and we were very sad to leave early on Tuesday morning and yet we looked forward to returning to our little hut. I had got almost everything I wanted on film except a good clear view of Mount Paget from Grytviken. In the four days we were there, the mountain refused to show her face once.

The next day, the launch dropped us off at Sorling Valley and we set off for Hound Bay. The few days' rest had obviously done us good because we were eager to reach Hound Bay hut, and to escape the rain and bitter cold we made it in two hours, instead of the three coming over. Once again, out came the Tilley lamps, off came the wet clothes and we got into our sleeping bags to warm up.

Wednesday morning dawned crystal clear with not a cloud in the sky so we went over to film the giant petrel nests we had found during our last visit. All the nests had large white fluffy chicks in them. The adults on two nests were of the very light colour variety, virtually completely white, just a few brown spots on them. We filmed the adults feeding their chicks and then went and climbed the hill behind the hut where, at last, we got some footage of Mount Paget in the distance.

Later that day we set out on the last lap home puffing and panting and stopping often to catch our breath. When we were about two-thirds of the way up the hill, a wind suddenly got up and I could see a thick bank of fog rolling down on to us. Within a few minutes, our visibility, which until then had been limitless, was reduced to fifty feet. Just before the fog hit us, I got out my compass and took a bearing on the pass to Luisa Bay so at least I had some idea of which direction to go. We plodded slowly on up the hill, checking with the compass every few minutes, hoping the fog would clear. It began to rain and grow very cold. Occasionally we sat on a rock to watch the thick solid fog float past us, wondering whether we should struggle on blind or turn back for the hut. We both wanted to get back to St Andrew's Bay, so we checked the map and compass and went on a little further. Finally we arrived at the top of the pass. At least we thought it was the top, but the fog was still thick and we could see little. We decided to try to find some shelter and wait for a while, hoping the weather would improve and let us continue on our way. We huddled down behind a few small rocks that barely gave us shelter, our woolly hats pulled well down, anoraks and gloves on, wet, cold and frustrated by the weather. For an hour or more we sat there shivering, certain now that the fog was getting worse. Eventually, I got fed up and worked out a bearing to get us safely back to the hut at Hound Bay. We really had no choice. Far better to return to the hut than spend the night out in the cold.

I knew that Grytviken would be expecting me on the radio at St Andrew's Bay that night and I hoped they would realise that the weather had delayed us. Anyway, there was nothing I could do about it, so on went the Tilley lamps again, off with the wet clothes and into our sleeping bags to warm up.

Next morning, it had stopped raining but the clouds were still very low and thick. I could see that the pass from Hound Bay to Sorling Valley was just out of the clouds and I could also see the Nordenskjold Glacier which had been hidden from view yesterday. It seemed worth a try, so once again we packed, cleaned out the hut and tried for St Andrew's Bay for the second time.

180

We climbed the long hill to the pass to Luisa Bay in only an hour, the clouds swirling round our heads. This time we cleared the top and started descending into Luisa Bay. We could see the fresh-water lake several hundred feet down and headed for it. We had a rest by the lake and stared up at the higher pass that led into St Andrew's Bay which we could just see below thick cloud. Every now and then the clouds would lift for a few minutes and we could see our route clearly. We decided to keep going until we reached the cloud base and then sit tight until a break came in the clouds. We knew that once over the pass we could reach the hut even if the clouds did come down again. We would be on home territory and knew nearly every stone on the other side.

So on we climbed, sweating in the chilled air, stopping eventually at about one thousand feet, where we met up with the clouds. We had only another two hundred feet to go to the pass but we had to wait for a break to show us the way. It was damp and cold sitting in the clouds and we longed to get home to the warmth of the hut, a hot wash, clean clothes and something to eat. We sat huddled together watching the clouds inches above our heads, praying for a break. After twenty minutes it came – the clouds started to lift and we were up in a flash, climbing as quickly as we could as the clouds rose slowly above us. Up and over the top we struggled and started working our way across the steep scree slope, slowly and carefully, checking each foothold. It was while we were half-way across the slope that the clouds came down again, thick and damp, reducing visibility to only a few yards, but we knew our way now and we were as good as home. Having crossed the slope, we came out onto the high ridge that overlooked St Andrew's Bay. We stood with the clouds all around us and heard the king penguins calling to each other in their colony down below and the sound of the surf breaking on the beach. I knew that if we followed the sound of the penguins and the surf, we would be heading towards the hut. So off we went, stopping every now and then to check our bearings.

At five hundred feet, we stepped out of the clouds and there, directly below us, was the hut and way off in the distance, the penguin colony. How good it was to be home again.

We took a few days to recover, but as it was now nearing the end of February, I was anxious to get on with my filming. We had only about six weeks left on South Georgia before the *Bransfield* came to collect us, or so I thought. I particularly wanted some moon shots and also some dawn shots of penguins on the beach.

In early March, the moon rose right in the centre of the bay at about ten p.m. It was absolutely beautiful. To reach the beach, we had to cross the still deep, but not so swift melt stream of the Heaney Glacier. I thought it was too risky, at night, to walk over the glacier for fear of slipping into one of the many holes or cracks. Because we never knew if the night was going to be clear, Annie and I would get ready for bed anyway – a wash and change into our pyjamas and then sit and wait for the moon. As soon as we saw the moon rising, we would strip off the bottom parts of our pyjamas and put on waterproof trousers and anoraks. Armed with torches, we would walk down to the melt stream and, with cameras held high, gasping as the icy water crept higher and higher, we would slowly cross over onto the beach. Once on the sandy beach, we would stop and rest, waiting for the numbing cold in our legs and feet to ease. For a half hour or so, we would quietly walk along the beach filming groups of penguins asleep, silhouetted by the moon.

The dawn shots took three weeks to obtain and meant getting up in the dark at four a.m. to be down on the beach in time for the first light to appear. As the sky slowly began to turn pink, the penguins on the beach would begin to stir themselves, wandering down to the water's edge and having a quick dip, playing and splashing in the surf before relanding. The snow-covered mountains surrounding the bay turned a beautiful shade of pink as the red sun rose over the horizon. Slowly the penguins would start to walk along the beach towards the north end of the bay where their launching rock was situated. There they would gather in huge numbers, standing around, preening and even having a quick snooze. The launching rock, or Rocky Point, as we called it, was a whole mass of rocks jutting out into the sea, the last one sloping gently down into the water. The kings would gather on these rocks, spending hours lazing around before one of them would finally decide to walk down the slippery seaweed-covered rock to flop into the sea.

Our next major excitement was the return of HMS *Endurance* in mid-March. This visit was particularly special because on board the Naval ice-patrol ship were my parents. It would also be *Endurance*'s last visit to South Georgia, as she was due to be scrapped at the end of the season. My parents had been given the invitation of a lifetime to join *Endurance* for three weeks in the Antarctic and to visit South Georgia, Faraday, Rothera and a few other foreign scientific bases. They went down to 68 degrees south, steaming into the thick pack-ice and among towering icebergs, flying around in helicopters, visiting the bases and having a wonderful time on board. On one base, a husky dog ate my mother's fur gloves. On another occasion, on board *Endurance*, just as Nick Barker stepped out of his cabin to do the 'Rounds', the ship gave a violent roll. My parents were standing not far away and my father put out his hand to support himself and accidentally leant on the knob of the fire extinguisher fixed to the wall. It exploded into life, squirting out foam all over the newly polished passage and an unfortunate man standing to attention nearby. My mother, incapable of controlling her laughter, dived back in to her cabin. Papa and some of the other men desperately tried to turn the extinguisher off and Nick Barker, trying not to laugh, turned round and went back into his cabin to wait for the mess to be cleared up.

HMS *Endurance* called me up on the radio on the evening of 14 March. They would be with us the following day. There the two of us were, living in a tiny wooden hut in the middle of nowhere on an Antarctic island and my parents were about to drop in. If only I had some dehydrated cucumber sandwiches to give them. Hardly able to contain our excitement, Annie and I scrubbed out our little hut, washed our hair and clothes and, once again, rummaged around for our skirts and shirts.

The day of their arrival, 15 March, dawned dull with low cloud, but, thankfully, calm. I sat in the hut quite unable to believe that my parents would be landing shortly, jumping at every sound and movement outside. At 10.30 a.m. *Endurance* called us up on the radio and I stared at it in delight as my mother suddenly came on the air. She told me that she and Papa were just about to climb into the helicopter and they would be with us in half an hour. Sure enough, at eleven we heard the helicopter engine. We fell over each other in our excitement to get out of the hut, grabbing cameras, film and lenses to film this historic occasion. The huge Union Jack flew proudly and this time the helicopter made a perfect landing.

I filmed my parents in their all-in-one bright orange flying suits, getting out of the helicopter and walking towards me and then down with the camera I threw my arms round my mother and held her very tight. Having helped them out of their suits, we took them into the hut and with mugs of steaming coffee in our hands, chatted happily for the next hour.

They had brought with them from England a large box of gifts for Annie as belated birthday presents and also a box of food from Stanley. Once the coffee was finished they were eager to be shown around and see the wildlife. On the beach, the penguins obligingly came to stare curiously up at my mother so that she got some lovely shots of them. She wasn't so keen on the massive bull elephant seals that were lying about shedding their skins. They were too big, ugly, smelt and made rude noises, she thought, but the albatross chicks she found enchanting.

How we pushed and pulled my parents up the steep tussock cliffs to the nests, I shall never know. It is not advisable for someone who has a 'dicky' heart and suffers from vertigo as my mother does, but she was determined to get there at all costs. Once there, she snuggled up to the chicks, photographing them and gently stroking their fluffy down.

Back at the hut for lunch, we started to get out the ration biscuits, butter and pastes when my mother suddenly produced a sausage – a real sausage – after all those months of meat granules. *Endurance* had provided a packed lunch and as they could see that Annie and I were drooling at the mouth over their lunch of cold sausages and sandwiches, my parents very kindly agreed on a swop. A fair swop, I thought! So while they battled with our ration biscuits, we sat back in ecstasy stuffing cold sausages into our mouths.

For the afternoon, we went and visited the king penguin colony. All the melt streams were too deep and swift to cross so we had to go by way of the glaciers. Neither parent had walked over a glacier before, so it was quite exciting and new. However, the glaciers were in a treacherous state with a very slippery surface owing to recent rain, and the going was slow and a little dangerous, but there was no other way of getting to the colony. My parents were amazed at its vast size and the mass of penguins packed tightly together with chicks of all sizes. I wish they had been able to see it all on a lovely sunny day with all the snow-covered mountains in view, instead of on a wet, cloudy, dull day.

In the evening, just before darkness a boat came to take us all back to *Endurance* which had now sailed into St Andrew's Bay and anchored there for the night. *Endurance* had spent the day at Royal Bay collecting the Joint Services Expedition who were returning home. As usual, Annie and I slept in the sick bay (now known as the Tarts' Parlour) and greatly appreciated the available shower. Annie booked a telephone call to her mother in England while the rest of us had drinks in Nick Barker's cabin. We had a lovely evening, with a huge buffet in the wardroom given by my parents for all on board.

I was very happy to have my mother with me at St Andrew's Bay. I hadn't seen her for six months and it was a lovely opportunity for Annie and me to have another woman to talk to. We had seen very few people during those six months and, with the exception of Mavis Hunt, they had all been men. Somehow, with my mother there, we were able to talk about the gentler side of life – the delicacy of the tiny plants, the solitary beauty of the icy peaks, the endearing fluffiness of the tiny albatross chicks. These were all things which we seldom discussed with men. It might have made us appear soft. On a more practical level, we plied her with ideas for cooking our meagre meat rations. 'We know of forty-three ways of cooking meat granules. Tell me one more way, just one,' begged Annie.

Next day, Mama and Annie went round to Grytviken with *Endurance* while Papa and I remained behind quietly discussing how the film was going and what I still needed to photograph. His help, advice and encouragement over the film were invaluable. I packed up every inch of exposed footage I had taken so far and gave them to him along with the filming notes to take back to England with him. A wise thing to have done, as things turned out. Papa and I had a lovely day together revisiting the seals, albatross and penguins. While we were walking along the beach, a pair of humpback whales suddenly surfaced only a few hundred yards away. In all the months I had been at St Andrew's Bay, it was the first sighting of whales. They were so close that we could clearly see the barnacles on their faces. It was a marvellous sight. We sat down and watched them for fifteen minutes before they finally dived and swam away.

That evening, the weather cleared and my parents were able to see the mountains and glaciers in all their glory. Tony Ellerbeck, one of the helicopter pilots, offered me the chance of going up to take some aerial shots and so, strapped into a safety harness, with my feet dangling through the open door, I was able to get some direct overhead shots of the glaciers and the penguin colony.

It had been a marvellous trip and the only sadness was that it was time for my parents to go. None of us knew then that the peace of South Georgia was soon to be shattered. Had we known what was ahead, Annie and I would probably have taken off then and there. As it was, we stood waving sadly until the helicopter was out of sight and darkness fell. Then we took down the Union Jack, little realising that, even then, the Argentinians must have been just round the corner.

11

'DEFEND IF YOU ARE PROVOKED'

The very first sign of trouble came on the evening of 19 March 1982. Twirling the knob of my radio, I suddenly picked up a very clear English voice reading out a lot of numbers. We locked into the frequency and sat listening, wondering who the voice belonged to. Suddenly, I knew.

'It's Steve Martin from the Grytviken base,' I said to Annie, 'but what on earth is he doing reading out numbers? And who is he talking to?'

'Do you think it's some kind of code?' asked Annie.

Just at that moment, Steve paused and then said, '*Endurance, Endurance*, did you receive that clearly? Over.'

This left us more puzzled than ever. Why was Steve sending a coded message to *Endurance*?

We felt a little perplexed but there was nothing we could do except sit and wait, the silence in the hut broken only by the hissing of the Tilley lamp. A few minutes later, Steve was on the radio again, this time to Dr Laws, Director of BAS, who was touring the bases on the BAS ship *Bransfield*. I was a little surprised when Steve, having spent half an hour sending a long coded message to *Endurance*, told Dr Laws in plain English that an Argentinian ship had anchored at Leith Harbour and a party of thirty-five Argentinian scrap-metal merchants and ten Argentinian naval personnel had landed at Leith whaling station. The Argentinians had raised the Argentinian flag and with the fire-arms they had brought with them were shooting reindeer and other wildlife for food.

My immediate reaction was one of fury that they should shoot the reindeer. These beautiful creatures had been brought out to South Georgia by the Norwegians at the beginning of the century. It had taken them only two years to adapt to life in the southern hemisphere and though they had run away from us when we had first arrived at St Andrew's Bay, they had gradually become used to us and learned to trust us. Now men with guns had arrived to break that trust. The BAS team at Grytviken had asked the Argentinians to remove their flag and to stop shooting the animals and though they had acceded to the first request, they had continued shooting reindeer.

Angry and puzzled by the whole thing, we stayed glued to the radio, but failed to pick up anything else except more coded messages. At midnight we gave up and went to bed.

For the next few days, Steve came on the radio regularly to tell us what was going on. London, he said, was taking a dim view of the whole thing and from now on a special channel – Channel 13 – was to be kept open all day for us to report to if we saw any ships, aircraft or personnel that obviously had nothing to do with BAS. It seemed that things were getting serious. Next day, we heard that the Argentinian ship had steamed out of Leith Harbour but had left behind a party of men and two small boats. We were thrilled also when we heard that *Endurance* had been recalled to the area, although I wondered what had happened to my parents – they had been due to sail with her all the way to Montevideo. Perhaps now the Ministry of Defence would at last wake up to the important role *Endurance* had to play in the South Atlantic area, being the only naval presence there and the only naval ship capable of going into the ice.

It was now the end of March. The brief summer months were over and the winter was slowly and relentlessly creeping in on us. The temperature rarely managed to struggle above freezing and the snow, though slushy and light was falling most days. We had about another two weeks of filming, we reckoned, before the BAS ship *Bransfield* came to collect us. During those last weeks, I hoped to get on film the blizzards and heavy snowstorms that I knew would descend on the island during the winter.

When, eventually, we did get out to film the blizzards, we found ourselves cursing and swearing as the snow fell on the lenses and the viewfinder became totally blocked so that I couldn't see a thing. Later on, when the temperature sank well below freezing, the on/off switch on the camera would frequently freeze solid and I would have to go back to the hut to thaw out the equipment.

On 24 March, we sat down to our usual meal of dehydrated meat. Yesterday it had been dried beef, today it was dried mutton, tomorrow it would be dried curry something and after that we would start all over again. Not surprisingly, because we were always hungry, every bit of dried meat, no matter what it was, tasted delicious. Just as we were about to start eating, we picked up the sound of an engine. Although chilled by the thought that the Argentinians were only twenty miles north of us, we rushed out of the hut and stood staring out to sea. In the advancing darkness, we just managed to pick out the navigation lights of a helicopter – and it sounded like the buzz of a Wasp. I rushed back to the hut and returned with the Tilley lamp, swinging it to and fro. To our delight, the helicopter, still a mile or so out at sea, replied by flashing its landing light on an off and then went away. It was comforting to know that *Endurance* was again near at hand.

A few days later, one of *Endurance*'s helicopters suddenly shot round the north end corner of the bay and landed by the hut. A very pleasant surprise. The pilot, Tim Finding, and his observer, Bob Nadin, asked us both if we would like to fly back with them to *Endurance* and have lunch with Nick Barker and return to the hut by evening. As we were fairly up-to-date with all our work, we said we would love to and after a quick cup of coffee and struggling into our bright orange flying suits, life jackets and headphones to protect our ears, we took off for *Endurance*. Although the weather was lousy, I did a bit of aerial filming out of the open door, ending up with partially frostbitten hands by the time we got to *Endurance*.

She was anchored in East Cumberland Bay, just off Grytviken base, and Nick was waiting for us as we landed on the flight deck, with his usual delightful smile and equally warm embrace. Once we had got out of our flying gear and I had recovered from the agonising pain of the circulation returning to my fingers, we went up to his cabin.

Over a drink he told us what was going on. Davidoff, an Argentinian scrap metal merchant, had signed a contract in 1979 with the Edinburgh shipping firm, Christian Salvesen, to remove all the scrap at Leith whaling station valued at millions of pounds. If Nick had a sneaking suspicion of what was to follow, he didn't tell us. Both he and Rex Hunt had wanted to take a firm line with the Argentinians at Leith, go in there and order them off, by force if necessary. It should be understood that while the Argentinians were at Leith quite legally, they had come ashore with arms and had refused to go through normal immigration procedures at Grytviken. Further, they had illegally raised the Argentinian flag. London, however, at the eleventh hour, had ordered *Endurance* not to go to Leith while they tried to sort out the problem through diplomatic channels. *Endurance* was told to anchor off

189

Grytviken harbour and to await further instructions. My parents, Nick said, had left the ship at Stanley to fly home from there.

All that *Endurance* could do was to take over from the BAS men and keep a sharp eye on the Argentinians at Leith. Every morning, at first light, one of the helicopters would fly low along the coast and land two Royal Marines on Grass Island, just two miles from Leith in the middle of Stromness Bay, to watch and report by radio every move the Argentinians made. Just as darkness descended, the helicopter would return to pick up the men for the night. During the day, the helicopters would fly over certain areas of South Georgia checking on any other sign of Argentinian presence. It was just as well they did. Lying eighteen miles out from Leith, they came upon the *Bahia Paraiso*, an Argentinian ice-breaker.

Although telexes flew between London, Buenos Aires, Stanley and *Endurance*, I thought the only two people who were taking it seriously were Rex Hunt and Nick Barker. To everyone else it all seemed rather exciting.

We stayed on *Endurance* for the night, borrowing two pairs of Nick's pyjamas which greatly amused the sailors. Nick had especially asked us to stay on board, perhaps to help the slightly flagging morale of the men, but also so that he could keep an eye on us for his own peace of mind. For the next few days, the helicopter flew us back to St Andrew's Bay each day so that I could get on with my work, and then brought us back to the ship in the evening. We listened regularly to the news broadcasts as South Georgia was now heading the world news. I suggested to Annie that she ring her mother who might be worried about the rapidly deteriorating situation.

To make it harder for anyone to eavesdrop, Annie used the very expensive satellite telephone system which allowed her to dial home directly. Without giving names or places, she quickly and calmly told her mother not to worry and that we hoped to be home soon. Little did we know!

Sunday, 28 March dawned a dull and bitterly cold day with a few odd snow flakes swirling in the sky. Being a Sunday, it was decided to hold a service in the little chapel at Grytviken whaling station. Only about twenty people went to it, which I thought was a little sad when perhaps we all needed, at that time, a few prayers answered. It was a service I shall never forget. The chapel bell echoed among the surrounding mountains and the organ was played by one of the officers, while we sang our hearts out to 'The Lord Is My Shepherd' and 'Eternal Father'. The pulpit was covered in a huge Union Jack and Nick stood in the pulpit to read out the prayers. It didn't last long, half an hour at the most, but it was a moving service and those of us who prayed did so with all sincerity.

That afternoon, Nick gave the ship's company a chat over the ship's television video system. He asked the men to be careful when they rang their families in the UK and not to give away any useful information. They were very low on fuel, he said as well as food, drink and cigarettes, as there hadn't been time to stock up when in Stanley. Food on board was already being rationed. There were no cooked breakfasts, lunch was a cup of soup or a bread roll and there was only a main course for supper. A few people were going to lose a little weight!

The BAS ship, the *John Biscoe*, which had brought us down from Rio was now in the Argentinians' bad books. Because *Endurance* was stuck at South Georgia, *Biscoe* had been asked by Rex Hunt to go to Montevideo to collect the new party of Royal Marines who were due to start their one-year stay in the Falklands. Under normal conditions when the new detachment of forty Royal Marines arrived, the old detachment would have left, but Rex Hunt was getting more and more worried about the deteriorating relationship between Britain and Argentina so he wisely decided to keep the old detachment with the new one to swell the possible fighting force from forty to eighty men. The *John Biscoe* was then ordered to steam back to Britain as quickly as possible to get away from the Falkland Islands and South Georgia, as she was a civilian ship and totally unarmed.

Nick decided to steam up the coast so that the two helicopters could scout around and make quite sure that, apart from the *Bahia Paraiso*, there were no other Argentinian ships about. The day was bitterly cold and very dull with low-lying clouds that didn't help the pilots who had had a very tiring day flying up and down the coast, occasionally darting back to the ship to refuel.

For Annie and me it was all rather exciting as we watched the small detachment of twenty-two Royal Marines on board uncover the two 20mm guns and load up the magazines with ammunition. No one pretended that those guns were large, they weren't, but they were all she had, apart from the air-to-surface missiles on her helicopters. This made *Endurance* and her crew that much braver as she was quite prepared to go anywhere and do anything.

As we were slowly steaming past the entrance to Leith Harbour on our way back to Grytviken, the *Bahia Paraiso* suddenly appeared out of the mist and drizzle, obviously wanting to make sure that we didn't sneak in and attack their men there. Nick took the opportunity of trying to talk to the captain and in awful Spanish he passed on a few

191

pleasantries like 'Good day' and 'Goodbye' which, to our surprise, were acknowledged.

We had a slightly nervous few minutes back at Grytviken harbour when the reverse gear on *Endurance* failed. Some very nasty-looking rocks loomed nearer and nearer while the two anchors were hurriedly lowered and as soon as they grabbed the bottom, the anchor winch brakes were slapped on. Smoke poured from the two winches as the sailors desperately tried to stop the forward motion of the ship. I felt helpless standing up on the bridge as the ship swung past the rocks before being finally halted by the anchors. What a disaster it would have been if *Endurance* had hit them and been holed. Nick remained cool throughout.

Annie and I left *Endurance* on 30 March and flew back to St Andrew's Bay via the glaciers and mountain tops so that I could get some more aerial shots. We were sad to leave *Endurance* and yet pleased to be back again at our hut in total peace and quiet, although the whole situation was rapidly crumbling around us. We sent short messages to our families before leaving *Endurance* to tell them we were both returning to St Andrew's Bay and that we were well and that they should not worry about us. Listening to the BBC news on the radio, it sounded to me as if the whole thing was on the point of explosion, at least so far as South Georgia was concerned. Nothing had happened yet in the Falkland Islands.

The next day was dull and wet and we spent most of it listening to the radio. Rumours were flying everywhere. It was thought that there were six Argentinian military ships round South Georgia. I found this hard to believe although I suppose it was possible. We spent a lot of time looking out of the door of our hut to check the horizon, but we never saw anything. It was very difficult for us to understand fully the gravity of the situation. There we were in our tiny hut with not a soul in sight, no ships, no planes, no troops – just thousands of penguins, seals, albatross and reindeer for company. It was impossible to believe that troops might storm up the beach to our hut pointing guns at us. The world was going mad. Britain didn't go to war. This was 1982 and we were all supposed to be civilised. Why couldn't everyone just sit down and talk calmly about the problem in an adult manner? We, after all, were only here for the penguins.

That evening, when I went on the radio to Grytviken, I was rather amused when the radio operator told us that South Georgia was still British. We all had a laugh. Perhaps a slightly nervous laugh? Had we known it, we had only three days to go before the British flag was torn down. It all seemed so unreal. There was constant talk of warships, submarines and troops gathering in southern Argentina and yet we just kept living our normal quiet lives, though underlying the normality was an ever-present tension.

One afternoon, with a blizzard blowing up outside, we decided to spend some time checking over our cameras. Apart from our lenses, Annie had two cameras and I had three. My Arriflex, although the noisiest and heaviest, was the one I used most. The Bolex, which is lighter and smaller, I tend to keep for use without a tripod and my Eclair is silent and therefore very suitable for use in an enclosed space such as a hide. All the lenses needed constant attention as they were exposed to such harsh weather conditions. They were often coated in seaspray and salt which had to be cleaned with chamois leather and a special solution. I had another handy gadget full of compressed air which got rid of tiny specks of dust and this I used together with an anti-static gun which had to be fired directly at the lens. If you made the mistake, as I did, of getting your hand in the way, you got quite a painful shock.

I was just starting work on the last camera when suddenly, I heard a scream coming from outside. I rushed out into the blizzard, fearful of what I might find. Down the slope in the wind tumbled the lavatory roll in a great gust of tangled pink tissue with Annie in hot and angry pursuit, her trousers still down around her ankles, while a group of startled penguins scattered out of her way. Life was, indeed, continuing as normal.

April 1st dawned sunny and calm with fresh snow lying everywhere, the sort of day when one feels good to be alive. Everything sparkled in the sunlight, the island looked clean and healthy. There wasn't even much news on the radio to dampen our spirits. It was, of course, the lull before the storm. We went out to do a bit of filming. With each passing day the chicks looked more like the chicks we had filmed when we had first arrived in October. The gap was rapidly closing.

We didn't know it, but the night of April 1st was our last night alone together at St Andrew's Bay.

It was still a source of amazement that Annie and I had proved such good company for each other. The explanation is probably that we both quite enjoy the solitary life, me more so than Annie perhaps. Very occasionally, I think how nice it might be to be married and lead the cosier life of a housewife, but that's only when I'm tired or fed up. I can see that it's perfectly possible for me to meet the right man one day but somehow I never seem to be in England long enough to get to know anyone well enough to think about marriage. It's been like that

193

certainly over the last eleven years when I've had to learn to cope on my own – though that's not to say I want to be one of the boys. When there are men around, I like to be treated as a woman. That's why we were both always delighted when the Navy turned up!

The next morning was miserable, blowing hard, half rain, half snow. Suddenly there was a knock at the door. For a moment neither of us said anything, then I got up to open the door. Outside stood three wet, cold men, all laden with heavy rucksacks. They had been walking non-stop since daylight. Peter Stark, a meteorologist, Tony North, a marine biologist, and Myles Plant, a carpenter – all from BAS at Grytviken – squeezed into the hut, their sodden clothes, boots and rucksacks dripping puddles everywhere.

The Argentinians, they said, were on the point of invading the Falklands. Rex Hunt had sent a message the night before saying an Argentinian invasion seemed almost inevitable and that if the Falklands were invaded then the Argentinians would, almost certainly, invade South Georgia. *Endurance* had been ordered back from South Georgia and she was now making her way to Stanley, having left behind the Marines to guard Grytviken. Pete told us that when he, Tony and Myles had left the BAS camp at the crack of dawn, the Marines were busy setting up their defence positions, mounting machine-gun posts and arming their anti-tank guns. Pete had been asked to come down to us just in case the Argentinians should turn up unexpectedly and Tony and Myles had asked to come too as they did not want to get involved in any fighting at Grytviken. Two other BAS men had left Grytviken and gone to join two men already at the hut at Lyell Glazier, five miles north of Grytviken. There were also four BAS men at Bird Island and two men at Schlieper Bay. That left twelve BAS men who had taken refuge in the chapel at the old whaling station and Steve Martin, who had remained on base with the Royal Marines.

Annie and I listened in silence. Only fifteen miles over the hill all this was taking place! We both knew the Falklands well and most of the people who lived there. They were our friends. *Surely* the Argentinians couldn't be so damn stupid as to invade? Surely Britain would do something? What in the hell was going on? We switched on our radio and, sure enough, the first item was an unconfirmed report that the Falkland Islands had been invaded by Argentina. I stared at the radio in utter disbelief.

At one p.m., the BBC news confirmed the invasion. A local man in Stanley had managed to get a quick message out over the air which a radio ham in England had picked up. It seemed that at six o'clock that

194

morning, two thousand Argentinian troops had landed at Stanley, capturing the airport and the town. The eighty Royal Marines had put up an amazing fight against such overwhelming odds but after three hours Rex Hunt ordered them to surrender. The Argentinians had reported one man killed.

With the weather outside the hut continuing to rain and snow and with the winds blowing at forty mph, we stayed in the hut, listening to the radio and keeping a listening watch for Grytviken, wondering if Steve would come on to tell us what the future was for all of us on South Georgia. Would we be invaded? Would the Argentinians take us prisoner?

At 7.30 p.m., Steve came on the radio to report that the Argentinian ship, *Bahia Paraiso*, which for the last week had been lying eighteen miles off shore, had sailed into East Cumberland Bay during the afternoon and then turned round and sailed straight out again without doing anything. I think they were checking to see if there were Marines at Grytviken.

Endurance had left South Georgia in a hurry on the evening of 1 April, but had not made it to the Falklands in time for the invasion. Steve told us to remain calm and that if we came in contact with the Argentinians, to stress the fact that we were civilians and to demand to be treated accordingly.

That evening, when the three men had gone out to the tiny two-man mountain tent for the night, Annie and I tried to pick up Stanley radio. We were very surprised when it came over quite clearly. I got out my tape recorder and from then on recorded everything about the invasion. It was, after all, going to be of great historic interest. We heard Rex Hunt's final speech to the Falklands just before he was deported by the new Argentinian Military Governor.

'Dear friends,' he said, 'I am afraid I have not been given as much time to say farewell to you all as I would have wished, by speaking to you all personally, but the new Argentine Governor has kindly given me permission to send you this last message of good wishes and thanks for all your support in the two years I have served you. I shall never forget you and hope that we shall meet again some day. In particular, Mavis and I would like to say farewell to all the Government House staff who we were not able to see today. Goodbye and God bless you all.'

Both Annie and I had lumps in our throats and our eyes began to water. Dear God, I thought, what has happened to the Falklands? It was incredible to think that Port Stanley was now swarming with Argentinian troops, all armed, ordering everyone about left, right and centre. Would *we* be going through the same thing tomorrow? From Stanley, people sent messages out to their families and friends in the islands to tell them not to worry. Mentally, we ticked off their names, relieved to know they were OK. Then an Argentinian officer came on the radio and spoke in Spanish for a few minutes. As neither of us could speak Spanish, we hadn't a clue what he was saying. However, at the end of the speech it was explained to us all that it had been a memorial message for the Argentinians who had been killed today during the fighting. So, more than one Argentinian had been killed!

Finally, the announcer said, 'Just before we close down there are one or two things I would like to say. This station has been broadcasting continuously for twenty-seven hours and we would like to give our thanks to the personnel of Cable and Wireless for their help and the risk they took, and also I would like to say that probably during the night there will be movement of heavy goods vehicles and personnel carriers and the best thing is to stay at home, go to bed and have a good night's sleep and things won't look quite so bad in the morning. We hope we have been of service to you. I will hand you over now to Alexander, one of the Argentinian officers. I wish you all a good night.' Alexander said, '*Ilas Malvinas, Buenas noches.*'

Neither of us slept much that night. We lay awake listening to the howling wind outside and occasionally talking to each other. Perhaps the Argentinians would want us off South Georgia? If so, where would they take us, would they be nice to us? How long would it be before we saw England again? Next day, the *Bahia Paraiso* came on the air ordering South Georgia to surrender. Helicopters, they said, would be sent in. Steve's reply to this was to plead with the ship not to send in helicopters as there were British troops at Grytviken who had orders to defend the place. It was then that *Endurance* came up on the radio and sent a message to the Marines. Nick Barker's message to the Marines at Grytviken came through, 'Rules of engagement are as stated earlier this morning. Defend if you are provoked.'

After this, the radio went mad. The *Bahia Paraiso* tried to contact *Endurance*. *Endurance* refused to answer. For several hours all the BAS bases plus the field parties on South Georgia tried to contact Steve Martin at Grytviken. No reply. What had happened to the thirteen BAS men and twenty-two Marines? Were they still alive, were they still fighting or had they been taken prisoners? Then we picked up the *Bransfield* calling Red Plum. Red Plum! Who was that? We decided Red Plum must be *Endurance*'s code name. The message was to all on South Georgia from the BAS Director at Cambridge.

'Regret unable to pass on instructions sooner but situation has been confused stop your position fully appreciated here stop you should remain as cool and calm as you can stop Ministry of Defence and Foreign and Commonwealth Office do not consider that you are in danger stop you should co-operate fully with military governor including evacuation if this instruction stop in that case please do best to ensure that all BAS supported personnel at South Georgia 28 are evacuated stop we are considering whether voluntary evacuation is desirable but you should use your own judgement on the various options and we will support you stop in either case you should if practicable take with you what low bulk valuable equipment you can stop next of kin being kept informed as and when they enquire stop best wishes and good luck from all here stop please confirm message passed and received at South Georgia message ends.'

The four field parties on South Georgia made contact with each other to confirm that we were still on the island and well. We also contacted Signy Island, eight hundred miles south-east of us to tell them that we were all OK. At four p.m. the five of us at St Andrew's Bay got a bit of a fright when we suddenly heard a helicopter. The Argentinians were to the north and though the sound seemed to be coming from the south we were still nervous. Very low out over the water, we could just make out a camouflaged helicopter coming straight for us but with relief we recognised it as one from *Endurance*, though no longer painted its usual bright red. Now it was a dark, ugly war machine.

It hovered briefly twenty feet above our heads and I could clearly see Tony Ellerbeck, the pilot, give us a quick thumbs up and a smile while his observer dropped a tin out of the door which landed by our feet. The helicopter shot off and disappeared the way it had come. Inside the tin we found two messages and a bar of chocolate. The first message was from Nick Barker telling us that the *Bransfield* was continuing her schedule and still planned to collect us in two weeks' time, although the Argentinians might pick us up first! Tony's message said,

Dear Team,
Sorry we can't stop for tea!! I never did like postmen who threw the mail in the porch. Please don't tell anyone we are about, it might spoil the game. Hope you are both OK, don't worry.
All the best.
Much love Tony
PS Just in case you were filming, we have lost radio contact with Grytviken after they had been asked to surrender. If we stick around, we

197

will keep in touch. No casualties at Stanley, military or civilian and Rex and Mavis will be in UK by now. Love Tony

The BBC news confirmed that evening that Grytviken had been invaded by Argentina. The Argentinian flag was now flying at the base. I decided that until the Argentinians came to St Andrew's Bay *our* Union Jack would continue to fly when weather permitted. So far as we were concerned, South Georgia was still British.

Later that evening, while we were having a final cup of tea, Annie returned into the hut from the loo. Her face was white. 'There's someone out there.'

'How do you know?' I asked.

'I could hear them walking around. There's more than one. They circled the hut and then went round the back of it.'

We decided we would all go together to investigate. Outside in the dark we could hear nothing but the endless wind blowing. There had been a recent fall of snow and our feet crunched through it as we walked round the hut, nervous and tense. Nothing. Then Annie said, 'Listen, there it is again.' This time, we all heard it. Footsteps, maybe two or three, all moving round the other end of the hut. Quietly, we edged our way round to find a small herd of reindeer moving off, their hooves in the virgin snow sounding just like footsteps. It had been a bad moment and we all went back to have another cup of tea.

We now expected to be picked up by the Argentinians within the next day or so and Annie and I decided to start packing up. It was heartbreaking stripping our little hut bare of all our belongings and cramming them into our trunks. We had had six wonderful months on South Georgia and now everything was going horribly wrong. All my cameras were dismantled and packed carefully into their cases. Clothes, books and other personal belongings were packed into trunks. A few small essential items were set aside and packed into a kitbag as we hoped that when we were taken by the Argentinians they would allow us to take one bag each. Everything else – all my equipment – would have to be abandoned.

I thought about burying the exposed footage of film I had with me, but it didn't amount to much as, thank God, I had given everything to my father only two weeks before. In the end, I decided to pack the film in my kitbag and just hope that nothing would happen to it. The unexposed footage, I would leave behind. At one a.m. we had finished. We looked around the bare hut. The last thing we wanted to do was leave St Andrew's Bay as prisoners of the Argentinians. Depressed, tired and dirty we went to bed.

The next day, 4 April, one of *Endurance*'s helicopters paid us another visit. Landing a helicopter was always tricky. One of the many hazards was from birds flying into the rotor blades. Sadly, the reindeer had begun to move away, frightened by the constant coming and going of the helicopter and, in fact, after the first couple of days we never saw them again. Our visitors this time were Tim Finding and his observer Bob, who sat on the wooden platform outside the hut for fifteen minutes telling us what had happened the day before. The twenty-two Royal Marines at Grytviken had done an amazing job shooting down two helicopters. They also damaged a corvette. *Endurance* didn't know how many Argentinians had been killed, but suspected that the figures were far higher than the three officially announced. The Marines had fought off two hundred Argentinian troops for three hours before finally surrendering. The thirteen BAS men and all the Marines had been taken prisoners and were aboard the *Bahia Paraiso* now back at Leith.

We were immensely relieved to hear that the men were all OK, although sad for them that they were being held prisoner. Tim told us that *Endurance* was monitoring our radio, could hear us, but we were not to call her up as they did not want the Argentinians to know they were around. Instead we were to call up one of the field parties and pass on any information so that *Endurance* could pick it up. He warned us that the Argentinians almost certainly were monitoring our radio as well, so we had to be careful what we said. Although we could have gone on board *Endurance* we decided to stay in the hut, as we felt in many ways safer at St Andrew's Bay and thought it would be unfair on the ship to have five civilians on board, especially if they suddenly came under attack. The helicopter flew away again and that was the last we saw of *Endurance* for three long and lonely weeks.

The BBC news that day told us that a large naval force was being prepared and would soon leave England and head for the Falklands. This kept our morale high. News from Stanley said that everything had been closed, schools, businesses and bars until further notice and that driving was now on the right-hand side. Everyone had been ordered to stay in their houses and if anyone was caught out on the street they would face a penalty of fifteen days imprisonment and sixty days imprisonment for showing disrespect to either the Argentinian forces or flag. Typical, I thought. Argentina for years had promised always to treat the Falkland Islanders with respect, give them everything they needed and allow them to live the way they were used to. A good start!

We had the best radio for receiving the BBC, so each night Peter Stark or myself would call up the three field parties and read out all the news items. We realised how important it was to them and it would help keep up morale while we waited for whatever our future might be.

A message from Dr Laws, now back at Cambridge, said that plans were being made for our evacuation, but no details could be given as they were all top secret. Of all the field parties, the four BAS men at Lyell Glazier hut were the least comfortable, being in a damp and draughty wooden hut, eight foot square with limited food and fuel. Therefore, if the men considered it wiser to surrender to the Argentinian forces at Grytviken, Cambridge would understand.

On Monday, 5 April, two of them excelled themselves by walking five miles to a hidden position to observe Grytviken. No one knew what was going on at the base, how many troops were there or if they were in the surrounding area. They observed Grytviken for several hours, took a few photographs, returned to their hut and sent a message to Signy Island for forward transmission:

1. Grytviken was visited by us from side of Hodges (a mountain overlooking the base)
2. Military personnel seen around Shackleton House.
3. Argentinian flag flying over Grytviken.
4. Believe there to be two possible machine gun posts either end of Shackleton House.

The men at Lyell Glacier were asked repeatedly to state clearly their exact position when observing Grytviken and to give as much detail as they could of what they had observed. At first, this questioning from one of the other bases seemed a little odd. Why should they be so persistent? Then we realised that London or *Endurance* were probably listening in and that the information was going to prove quite useful. The Lyell Glacier men had done a tremendous job.

We had waited for four days for the Argentinians to come and pick us up and I was more and more convinced with each passing day that they had no intention of doing so. Living conditions in the hut were now becoming difficult. With five of us crowded into the hut, Annie and I were finding it hard to keep either ourselves or the hut clean. Finally, in desperation we asked the three men to go for a walk for an hour while we boiled some water, stripped off and had a good scrub outside the hut on a cold, grey day. Putting on clean fresh clothes was bliss and we felt quite cheerful again. I unpacked my main camera, fixed the solar panel back onto the roof of the hut and started to recharge the camera batteries. I still had a job to do and I wanted to finish it. From then on we went out filming when weather permitted.

We filmed some fantastic snow blizzards and white-outs with winds of over a hundred mph and fresh snow swirling around so that we could not tell the difference between the sky and the ground. Visibility was reduced to a few feet. I set up the camera, digging the tripod legs firmly into the ground and Annie filmed me walking out of the door of the hut holding the radio aerial so I wouldn't get lost and disappearing into the white-out ten feet from the hut. One strong gust of wind picked me up physically and threw me to the ground, but I managed to hold on to the aerial pole until it had passed. It was extremely difficult, almost impossible, to film in such conditions.

One very unpleasant thing that frequently happened was that after I had been filming for a time in sub-zero temperatures with the wind thundering round me, I got quite a severe ear-ache which made further work out of the question. To get ten seconds worth of film was a major feat. Even when we did manage a few feet, Annie would have to put all her weight down onto the tripod head so that it didn't take off with the camera.

We continued to listen to news from Britain, passing it on to the other field parties each evening. At one time, it was reported that *Endurance* had been sunk during the Grytviken invasion. We at St Andrew's Bay knew this was not true as we had had two visits from her helicopters since the invasion. As soon as *Endurance* heard the rumour, she sent a message back to London to inform everyone she was very much afloat and well.

BAS asked us to check our food and fuel supplies. We had no immediate food problem but only five weeks of fuel. The four men at Lyell Glacier had only three weeks' supply of food left and were also running low on fuel. On the evening of 6 April, Lyell Glacier radioed that they were going to walk to Grytviken the next day and surrender to the Argentian forces there. They would take with them a white flag and a letter to the Argentinian commander of the base.

This sudden turn of events worried BAS HQ. The Foreign Office was in touch with the International Red Cross and were hopeful that some sort of evacuation might be arranged for everyone. Surrender by one group might jeopardise these negotiations. I myself had felt it to be a mistake and was relieved when the men at Lyell Glacier agreed, after all, to wait a bit longer. It had been an unwise plan. The men would have been locked up in a room, no one would have heard anything and we would then have worried about them on top of all our other problems.

One night around 10 o'clock with heavy snow falling outside, we were in the hut listening to the news when we once again heard footsteps outside the hut. We all froze where we were. Pete and Myles were sitting on the lower bunk and Annie and I were at the table jotting down notes from the news. The footsteps stopped and we heard someone banging their boots against the wooden platform. Dear God, I thought, the Argentinians have arrived. The adrenalin shot through my body and my heart started racing. I first looked at Annie who was staring at me, pen poised over her note pad, and then I looked at the men. Both had stopped in mid-motion and were staring at the door. Suddenly, there was a knock on the door. Oh God, there really was someone outside. Again I looked at the men, but they hadn't moved an inch so, rather reluctantly, I got up and went to the door which was bolted from the inside. Before sliding back the bolt, I looked round and found Annie right behind me with the men still sitting on the bunk. Very slowly, very carefully, I opened the door.

The light from the Tilley lamp burst through the door, and instead of finding an Argentinian soldier pointing a gun at me, I found Tony North, grinning in the snow. We were not expecting him. He had left the hut earlier in the day to walk to Hound Bay hut to collect a few food items we were short of. Annie and I had been very grateful to him for going and he had intended to stay the night at Hound Bay and return the following morning. Poor Tony. I really laid into him because he had given us all an awful fright. Instead of being pleased and grateful to see him with his rucksack bulging with food, we growled at him saying he should have called out a warning. We had all aged about ten years in two minutes.

Signy Island informed us one evening that they had managed to contact a radio ham in England who could send short messages to our families. So for the first time since the invasion we sent very brief messages to say we were well. Within twenty-four hours Annie and I got a message back from my father saying he had received our messages and all were working hard for us.

Then came the bombshell. Argentina imposed a two-hundred-mile military zone around the Falklands and South Georgia and threatened to attack any British ship seen inside the zone. *Bransfield*, which had been on the way to collect us, was ordered to leave the area immediately – without us. The Ministry of Defence felt that the ship could easily be captured and held hostage and though the captain and BAS were not happy with the decision, they had to comply. The ship's message to us all ended, 'We ask for your understanding. Everything possible will be done in the UK to arrange evacuation and repatriation. We will be back next summer or earlier. My personal best wishes to you all. May your God be with you. Stewart Lawrence, RRS *Bransfield*.'

I think we all felt a bit more cut off the day *Bransfield* turned away from us and headed north. While we at St Andrew's Bay were in a bit of a daze at this news, the men at Lyell Glacier took a different view. To them, the situation was completely unacceptable. Within two weeks they would need more food, more fuel and new batteries for the radio. The *Bransfield* had been their only hope and now it was gone.

Lyell Glacier sent a message to the BAS headquarters at Cambridge: 'If we are not evacuated from South Georgia before the onset of winter, we feel our only course of action will be to give ourselves up to the Argentinian military who have already detained thirteen BAS personnel without disclosing their whereabouts for seven days and who are noted for their ignominious loss of civilians. We fear we will cease to be able to contact the outside world within a matter of days. We must say that we are both afraid and deeply concerned by the situation.'

Cambridge asked them, in reply, to remain at Lyell Glacier if they possibly could.

With the departure of the *Bransfield*, the strain we were living under got worse. Apart from anything else, every day, I had to open up the depot, drag out the large heavy metal cases which held my camera and other equipment and each evening I had to pack it all up again, lock the cases, carry them back to the depot and close the depot for the night.

The difficult thing was not knowing how long it was all going to continue. Our three guests had come expecting to stay only a few days and didn't really have adequate clothes for the rigorous winter that was now setting in. One evening, I happened to mention this over the radio, remarking that, in my opinion, they were not properly clothed. This caused uproar producing a lot of laughter and whistling down the radio. Some bright spark from one of the other bases said they were sure we would find some way of keeping each other warm if the need arose!

Now that we knew we would have to stay for some time yet, we got out another tent for the men. We had not used the larger tent before because it was damaged and it hadn't seemed worth repairing the tear if we were to be evacuated. The only suitable thing we could find to mend the rip was a long bandage from our medical box. Sitting outside, on a cold and windy day, Annie and I spent two hours sewing the bandage to the tent over the tear, hoping it would hold in a hundred-mph wind. The men were delighted, as they could now use the smaller tent to store their gear in, and could sleep in the larger one.

The weather now was very cold. Standing out in the wind, the temperature was around minus twenty and, while working outside, we had constantly to watch each other for signs of frostbite – the nose turning white is usually the first. Once, while out filming in a white-out, I found that even the hairs in my nose had frozen. On the whole, our feet stayed warm. Our hands were the problem. It was virtually impossible to do any sort of camera work without taking off our gloves. We usually wore three pairs. First, a silk pair which were very warm, then a pair of chamois gloves and, finally, a pair of padded mittens. All these had to come off while we were filming.

Threading the film had to be done with great care as the extreme cold made it brittle and the slightest kink would cause it to snap. Another regular problem was moving the head of the tripod which was operated by oil under pressure. When the oil thickened in the cold, the tripod head locked and the only thing to do was to go back into the hut and try to warm the oil.

Drying clothes had become an almost insuperable problem and meant we often had to work in sodden clothes. Indeed, the whole question of hygiene began to irritate us. For Annie, it was particularly hard to bear. The muddy boots, rucksacks and dripping clothes which always littered the hut nearly drove her mad. She is, by nature, a fanatically tidy person, and it became a joke the number of times she got down on her hands and knees to clean the floor or how often she would go out into the snowstorm to do the washing up. I knew exactly how she felt.

It was difficult for the men, as they had no work to do and nothing much with which to occupy themselves. Pete, however, decided to creosote the hut, ready for the long winter, then he dismantled the BAS depot at the back of the hut, threw away the rubbish and listed all the things that needed replacing.

In a way, the main burden fell upon Annie as she had the job of cooking for five people every day. I did the washing up and Pete took on the job of making lunch which was mainly packets of soup and biscuits. How I longed to get my teeth into something that I could crunch my way through. Tony and Myles had enormous appetites and cheerfully got through four or five bars of chocolate a day – and then raided the kitchen for extra biscuits. Very occasionally, we were able to supplement our sledging rations with some goodies such as custard powder or some Worcester Sauce.

When the Argentinians had been expected hourly, we had put up the shutters as blackouts, but it had made the hut dark and with fewer hours of light each day, we soon took them down again to conserve our failing fuel supply. On bad days, we all huddled in the hut, Tony and Myles lounging on Annie's bunk, me up on mine and Annie and Pete perched uncomfortably on two stools. On those sort of days, we probably didn't smile at each other as often as we should.

Sunday, 11 April was just another day with the wind howling off the glacier. Tuning in to the last broadcast of the day, I picked up something we had all missed. Checking on the calendar, I found it was true – Easter Sunday had come, and almost gone, without our noticing.

The Argentinian radio was still sending out edicts from Stanley, some of which were quite amazing. Every holder of a two-meter radio not located in Stanley must dismantle it and deposit the valves at a distance of at least three miles from their equipment.

All Annie and I could say to that was two fingers! The Argentinians were going to have to come to St Andrew's Bay if they wanted our radio. I most certainly was not going to trudge three miles up the Heaney Glacier and dump the radio valves. And in any case, we didn't have valves in our radios, we had crystals!

The news from Britain continued to tell us that the Task Force was getting nearer and nearer, and hardly a day passed without another ship of one sort or another joining in, swelling the numbers to sixty, then seventy and then eighty vessels. I didn't know we had that many ships. From the other side, we were told that Argentina was also preparing herself for war. Rumours said that some of her naval ships had left port and it was thought they were heading for South Georgia. It was admitted by Argentina that it would be difficult to defend South Georgia but they were going to try. Diplomatic talks were still continuing, but I don't think any of us now thought that any solution would be found in time to stop the imminent battle.

The men at Lyell Glacier were now getting even more desperate. They had been advised by BAS HQ that there were additional food and fuel supplies at a number of sites within walking distance of them, but, of course, they had already been out to these and found that, in fact, there wasn't as much food or fuel as everyone had first thought. We were becoming concerned for their morale.

It was now fifteen days since the invasion of South Georgia and on 18 April, we received our first bit of news that really cheered us up – the thirteen BAS men taken prisoner at Grytviken had arrived home in England safely. This somehow gave hope to those of us still stranded and we celebrated by having an extra long chat on the radio with all the other bases. In fact, the radio was one of the things that kept us going through those dark days. Tired and depressed as we were, we often found ourselves deep in discussion about some news item that had come over the World Service, but the programme that really got us laughing was *Just a Minute*.

That night, Signy Island went off the air. A fierce gale had blown across the island ripping the felting off the roof of the BAS hut. This had sailed through the air and brought down the aerials.

The men at Signy hastily put up a temporary radio aerial but the communications to us on South Georgia were very weak. Only by constantly repeating their message very slowly, and by us straining our ears for each word, were we able to understand what had happened. For forty-eight hours, our messages to Signy were reduced to very short transmissions simply saying that all field parties on South Georgia were well. We were very relieved when, after two days of frantic work repairing the damaged radio aerials, Signy Island came back on the air loud and clear and were connected, once again, to the outside world.

The next day, Tony and Myles decided to walk northwards to Hound Bay, about five miles away. They hoped to locate some food supplies which we knew were over there.

By now, the Task Force was near enough to call us up. For security reasons, we were told simply that 'other people' would be in touch. We all knew who the 'other people' were. It was getting quite exciting.

12

RESCUE

Life changed dramatically for all of us at St Andrew's Bay on Wednesday, 21 April. Tony and Myles had intended staying away only one night, but the weather worsened rapidly and we wondered if, in fact, they would manage to get back. With the two of them away, we had a bit more room to spread ourselves around the hut and spent much time listening to the radio. Eventually, Annie and I felt we needed a bit of air and while we were out on Rocky Point we spotted a ship, as I have described in the Prologue. We were more than a little relieved when the Wasp helicopter flew in from *Endurance* with Tommy Scott on board, to warn us that British troops were preparing to retake South Georgia.

The plan was to land SAS and SBS (Special Boat Squadron) troops at Hound Bay just north of us, and for the men to walk across to Sorling Valley. From there, rubber boats would be launched and the troops would paddle across Cumberland Bay East to Moraine Fjord under cover of darkness when they would land. *Endurance* knew that the troops could not possibly cross the three glaciers in between Sorling Valley and Grytviken, as all three were heavily crevassed and very dangerous at this time of year. From Moraine Fjord, the troops would find a suitable observation point and watch Grytviken for twenty-four hours, before returning to Hound Bay and back on board *Endurance* the way they had come.

We were told all this so that, should we see any troop or ship movements, we would maintain radio silence, and not give the game away to the Argentinians. A similar sort of operation was going to be mounted near Leith, where there were more Argentinian troops.

Our immediate concern was for Tony and Myles who were already at

Hound Bay. If the SAS men failed to recognise them, they stood in very grave danger of being shot at. Somehow or other the news of their presence had to be got to the SAS as quickly as possible. It was decided that the helicopter should return to *Endurance* immediately, taking Pete along as well. He had lived on South Georgia now for two years and knew the terrain well. He would be able to give a lot of useful advice to those planning the attack. As soon as he had grabbed a few things together, the helicopter took off, leaving Tommy behind with Annie and myself.

Annie and I listened to Stanley radio and felt a great sadness for the people there when we realised what they were going through. They had been told to be prepared for air-raid attacks and to keep away from the beaches because of the danger of land mines. With an additional 10,000 Argentinians billeted on the island, the water problem was becoming acute. What an awful time they were having. If only we could have cheered them up with the welcome news that our troops had already arrived on South Georgia. We were, in fact, the only people to know that a counter attack was imminent. Tony North and Myles Plant returned to St Andrew's Bay from Hound Bay at mid-day on 22 April. They had met a few of the SAS who had been landed by *Endurance*, and admitted that they had got a bit of a shock when they saw heavily armed troops coming ashore. They had been told to stay at Hound Bay hut for the night, but to return to St Andrew's Bay immediately the following morning. The falling snow had turned to sleet so the two men were soaked through by the time they reached us. They were surprised to find Tommy with us and I noticed a certain chilliness in their greeting. Tony seemed disappointed, and not a little jealous perhaps, that Pete had been chosen to go back to *Endurance* to advise the SAS. In fact, Tony would have had quite a useful contribution to make as well as he was a diver and had considerable knowledge of the waters round South Georgia.

We spotted *Endurance* twice that day. Once in the early morning, far out on the horizon, and again in the late afternoon with HMS *Plymouth*. They were only about five miles off shore and very close together. We all wondered what they were up to.

That evening Signy Island passed us the following message from Cambridge: 'To all field parties. Could you be packed and reasonably ready to leave at fairly short notice? End of message.'

This bit of information didn't come as much of a surprise to us at St Andrew's Bay, but it did wonders to the other field parties who had no idea what was going on. As it happened, we had all been packed and ready to go for the last four weeks. It seemed that Signy Island was now in radio contact with the Navy and we were all told to tune in to a frequency which the Navy could use too.

Again, for all of us this bit of information was very encouraging news. It meant that our ships were near to us and that, perhaps, our days under Argentinian occupation were soon to end. Super news. Next came a message for me from my parents.

'Cousin Dan died very peacefully yesterday. Everybody well and much love. Please acknowledge.'

I was very sorry to hear that Cousin Dan, who lived on the north Norfolk coast not far from my little cottage, had died and I duly replied: 'Please pass my deepest sympathies to Mary Athill. All well and much love.'

What I didn't realise was that this message about Cousin Dan had a very special significance for my mother in England. Having heard little from me for a few weeks and then only through BAS at Cambridge, she had become convinced that the messages she was receiving weren't from me at all, and that somebody was making them all up! Receiving the message for Mary Athill, however, proved that the message really was from me. Nobody else could know that Mary was Cousin Dan's daughter.

The Navy was now very near the point of confrontation. The 24th of April started for us just before dawn. The first sign of light in the sky didn't appear until nine. Annie and I were up and I had already been on the radio to the other field parties to say that all was well at St Andrew's Bay and that I had nothing to report. We had washed up and were doing the daily morning duties of cleaning out the hut, filling the Tilley lamps with paraffin, burning any rubbish and collecting water. It was a beautiful clear, very cold morning. Tony, Myles and Tommy were still in their tents, dead to the world. All of a sudden we picked up the sound of a helicopter. Flying very low, it shot round the corner of the bay and in a matter of seconds landed neatly by the hut. Out of the tents appeared three bleary-eyed heads. Tim Finding, the pilot, stayed in the helicopter with the engine running while Pete and Bob Nadin, the observer, jumped out and came over to the hut. Tommy was told to get dressed quickly as he was to go back to *Endurance*. In the few brief minutes while Tommy was packing, Bob told us that operations had not gone all that well, but the main problem was that an Argentinian submarine was lurking nearby. All the other British ships had moved away leaving *Endurance* to find the submarine and pick up the SAS and SBS still on South Georgia. There was no further time to talk and the helicopter with Tommy on board took off, leaving Pete once again with us.

Pete spent the next hour telling us what had happened. Things, indeed, had not gone well. Apparently, the SAS had originally wanted to land on the other side of South Georgia at King Haakon Bay and to follow Shackleton's route over the island to get into position to observe Leith. Both Pete and Nick Barker had told them that this was suicidal at this time of year when the weather was so changeable. They might start off on a beautiful sunny day, but in a matter of hours they could find themselves in a white-out with winds of over a hundred mph. Pete and Nick also felt the men did not have the necessary equipment for such a journey.

The SAS, however, wouldn't listen. They said that they were trained for this kind of work in Norway, but they failed to realise that Norway is nothing like South Georgia.

In the end, the SAS were flown in two Wessex helicopters, from RFA *Tidespring*, which landed them safely on Fortuna Glacier and then flew away. As the men started to cross the glacier, the weather began to close in. Within an hour, the SAS troops found themselves still on the glacier in a complete white-out with winds of over a hundred mph and visibility reduced to a few feet. There was nothing for it but to send a radio message to ask for the two helicopters to return and pick them up.

In a white-out, with snow swirling everywhere, it was impossible to distinguish the ground from the sky and the pilots were extremely brave to try, but they kept moving slowly, desperately looking for the trapped men and then, suddenly, they flew straight into the glacier. The machines had been flying very slowly so, although they were written off, the men on board were uninjured though considerably shaken. A Wessex helicopter from HMS *Antrim* was sent in and, by this time, the weather conditions were beginning to improve. The howling wind was dying down and the snow not falling so heavily. The men on the glacier had been able to climb inside the two crashed helicopters and get some protection from the biting cold.

The third pilot proved to be the hero of the day, repeatedly flying in and filling up his helicopter to capacity with frozen men and flying back to *Antrim*. Again and again, the pilot flew on to Fortuna Glacier collecting all the men. He deservedly earned the Distinguished Service Order for his bravery.

The third plan to observe Leith was rather surprising and even that operation did not go quite according to plan. HMS *Antrim* steamed right into Stromness Bay within three miles of Leith where the

Argentinians were. Several small rubber boats were dropped over the side of *Antrim* and SAS troops poured into them. The troops, using noisy outboard motors headed for Grass Island only two miles from Leith where an observation post was set up to spy on the Argentinians. The outboard engine on one of the boats broke down and the boat with four men in it drifted away. By the time Pete got back to the hut, the four men had still not been found although, as it happened, a day or so later they were found stranded on a tiny beach safe and well although cold and wet.

We were a bit stunned by Pete's account of the operations and also a little depressed and sorry at how things had gone so far. Now there was a new panic on. The previous night an Argentinian radio transmission from a submarine to Grytviken base had been picked up. This meant that the Navy was vulnerable to attack by a submarine at any time. The main concern was for the tanker *Tidespring* which Tommy had told us was in the area and, being full of fuel, was a floating bomb. *Antrim* and *Plymouth* immediately began to escort her well clear of the area to the east side of South Georgia. This left *Endurance* on her own to go and collect the SAS and SBS due back at Hound Bay and to try and find the submarine and sink it. We felt very sorry for *Endurance* and desperately worried for all the men aboard her.

Although weather over parts of the island was bad, we at St Andrew's Bay had a beautiful day – clear and very cold. Annie and I decided to do some much-needed washing and were by the little stream that runs near the hut, rinsing out the clothes, when Pete appeared at the door of the hut, pointing up into the clear blue sky: 'A plane, a plane!' I grabbed the binoculars and focused on it as it flew down the coast of South Georgia. It was an Argentinian Boeing 707 spy plane. We dashed into the hut, turned on the radio and transmitted blind to Bird Island repeating several times what we had seen. (We knew they wouldn't answer as it wasn't the normal chat time.) We knew *Endurance* could hear us although she wouldn't answer and it was really to her we were passing the information.

Late that afternoon, we saw *Endurance* passing St Andrew's Bay very close in to the shoreline. She had obviously sneaked in to pick up the SAS and SBS. Annie and I stood out on the Rocky Point as she passed us. We waved our hands and hats and were thrilled when she replied to us by flashing her signal lights, just to say hello!

That night from London came news of the first British casualty – a helicopter from HMS *Hermes* had been forced to ditch in the sea. The pilot had been rescued but the observer was still missing. Argentina reported that British troops had already landed on South Georgia. We were all a little amused when on a later news broadcast Argentina announced that British troops had not, after all, landed on South Georgia. Their reason for the sudden change of heart was because the weather conditions around South Georgia were so bad with high winds, heavy snow and freezing temperatures that it was impossible for troops to land. If only they knew. Argentina had obviously got her weather reports from Grytviken or Leith.

Sunday, 25 April was another beautiful sunny day. Strangely enough, we heard nothing all morning although we learned later that the Argentinian submarine, the *Santa Fe*, had been attacked at Grytviken harbour. Apparently it had sneaked into Grytviken on the previous evening, dropping off fifteen more troops as reinforcements, with ammunition, supplies and mail. At first light on Sunday morning she eased out of Grytviken heading for the open sea when she was spotted. The Wessex helicopter from *Antrim* found the submarine and dropped a depth charge by the *Santa Fe* which certainly shook her. The submarine immediately headed back for harbour. Then one of *Endurance*'s Wasp helicopters came in to attack, armed with air-to-surface missiles and piloted by Tony Ellerbeck and his observer, David Wells. They homed in on the *Santa Fe*, coming under fire from Argentinian troops at Grytviken. This attack was followed by further sorties by *Endurance*'s other Wasp, piloted by Tim Finding. Five hits on the submarine were reported. Now that the *Santa Fe* was safely out of the way and the element of surprise had gone, it was decided to attack Grytviken immediately.

At 2.14 that sunny Sunday afternoon we heard the first shell explode. At first we thought it was an avalanche and looked around the mountains surrounding St Andrew's Bay. Then we heard another explosion which, this time, seemed to come from Grytviken. Perhaps the Nordenskjold Glacier, the largest on South Georgia, was calving huge bits of ice into the sea? And then a third, fourth, fifth explosion, all in quick succession, again coming from Grytviken. We all looked at each other and immediately knew what was going on. 'Good God,' Annie said, 'Grytviken is being attacked by the Navy.' Myles and Tony shot off to their tent, grabbed their climbing boots and almost ran up the 1,200-foot ridge behind the hut from where on a clear day, we could just see Grytviken. Pete went down to the high tussock cliffs where the albatross nested to check the horizon for any ships. For a while, Annie and I sat by the hut listening to the shells exploding fifteen miles the other side of the mountains.

212

The explosions continued until 3.50, just over one and a half hours of almost constant firing and then, suddenly, it stopped.

Pete came back first and said that he could see nothing out to sea. Tony and Myles returned rather puzzled. They hadn't seen any ships or any of the shells exploding, even though they could see the base. At first we wondered if they had attacked Grytviken at all, perhaps they were attacking Leith or an Argentinian ship somewhere nearby? Later we were told that *Antrim* and *Plymouth*, three miles off, using their heavy 4.5 guns had bombarded Brown Mountain, which is opposite Grytviken base on the other side of the harbour. Their aim had been to show the Argentinians the fire-power of the Navy, in the hope that it would frighten them enough to surrender.

At four we heard on the BBC that the British had attacked an Argentinian submarine found in the South Georgia area. At six we heard that British troops had landed on South Georgia. But it wasn't until eight p.m. that we heard the news we had been waiting for – the Argentinian forces on South Georgia had surrendered. They had apparently put up little resistance. We jumped up and down in our tiny hut, cheering and shouting, 'Hurrah for the Navy!'

Pete went on the radio with the good news. We were especially keen to contact the men on Lyell Glacier and when they came up on the radio, we could hear that they were enormously relieved at our news. The chat on the radio became quite light-hearted – something it hadn't been for weeks.

'Lyell here. Yes, got all that Pete, great news, really good to hear we may be going home soon. Over.'

'Yes, I agree with you, Lyell. I expect you will see a helicopter come round to visit you and drop in a bottle of scotch. Over.'

'Yes, I hope so. If it is a really nice day tomorrow we may, in the afternoon, take a walk. Over.'

'I would not suggest you go over to Grytviken, Lyell, or take a wander at all until you receive confirmation that you can from the helicopters or ships or whoever are in the area. You might be mistaken for wanderers. Over.'

'Understood St Andrew's Bay. Over.'

'Yes, OK. I think that would be sensible and not to be seen poking heads over ridges.'

'St Andrew's Bay, this is Bird Island. That is certainly really marvellous news. I think if no one else can get a bottle of whisky to Lyell, then we will take orders from this end for drinks when we all get together again. Over.'

'I will take you up on that, Bird Island. Over.'

'By the way, Pete, I don't think Lyell would be mistaken for wanderers. They are about three feet tall, white and have a wing span of eleven feet. Over.' (Wanderer is the everyday name for the wandering albatross.)

'Well, from what they have been eating at the Lyell, they may well look like that. Over.'

We went on chatting, telling jokes, laughing and discussing what we would do when we got home. Signy Island called us up and then we tuned in to the BBC radio and listened to 'Calling the Falklands' and to the speech Mr Nott made outside No. 10 Downing Street when he officially announced the Argentinian surrender of South Georgia. We were all very excited and relieved to know that our families now knew that once again we were under British rule and we would soon be coming home. Mr Nott also read out the wonderfully old-fashioned telegram to the British Government informing them of the re-taking of the island. It read:

> Be pleased to inform Her Majesty that the White Ensign flies alongside the Union Jack on South Georgia. God save the Queen.

Then there was a short announcement that thirteen British scientists and two women film-makers on South Georgia were said to be safe. The British Antarctic Survey said it had been in touch with the island by radio and were told the scientists were well. Buenos Aires denied that their troops had surrendered on South Georgia and, in fact, stated that their men were still fighting fiercely against the British and resisting the attack. We all smiled when we heard this announcement.

We celebrated well into the night, our little hut shaking under the cheers, toasts to the Navy, SAS, SBS and Royal Marines. What a wonderful fighting force we had. Lyell Glacier celebrated with a cup of tea and a bar of chocolate each. Bird Island and Schlieper Bay still had some alcohol with them, and the three men at St Andrew's Bay broke open the last bottle of whisky. Annie gulped down her last mouthful of brandy and I made do with a cup of hot chocolate. We tuned in to Stanley radio that evening to find out how the Argentinians were taking the loss of South Georgia. However, Stanley radio reported that the communication link from the islands to the mainland had broken down – how very unfortunate! So there was no news that night from Buenos Aires.

Next morning, I stood at the door of the hut straining to hear the sound of engines. I'd picked up on the radio that a helicopter would be calling on the men at Lyell with supplies round about 10 a.m. It was now eleven a.m. and we should surely be next on the list. Then across the glacier, I saw the beginnings of a storm starting to blow and within half an hour we were in the middle of a white-out. Whatever the plans might be, there would be no helicopter landing this morning. This was disappointing after the celebrations of last night, but there was nothing much we could do.

'How about doing some filming to celebrate our first day of freedom?' said Annie.

'You'd be mad to go out in the middle of this,' said Myles. 'Those winds are about a hundred mph.'

We probably were mad, but we were feeling restless and needed to do something. Outside we had to cling to the guy ropes as we tried to move away from the hut. In a matter of seconds, I noticed that the back of Annie's jacket had become completely caked in snow as it blasted right at us. I wanted to take some film of the hut but was anxious not to move too far away, in case I lost sight of it. I tried to set up the camera but found it impossible to stand upright and we had to crawl along on our hands and knees. The force of the wind whipped all the breath out of my body and I had to sign to Annie that we should give up. In an hour, we had only managed to get about six minutes filming.

Next day, the snow had died down but the gale was still blowing. A message came from Grytviken to say that we should stay put for a bit longer while they got things straight. The beaches were strewn with landmines which had to be defused and there were nearly two hundred prisoners at Shackleton House who also had to be sorted out.

We heard also that Leith had surrendered. *Endurance* and *Plymouth* had steamed into Stromness Bay and over the radio Nick Barker ordered Captain Astiz, the Commander, to surrender. The night before, Nick had asked Captain Astiz to allow the scrap-metal merchants to leave Leith and walk over to the old whaling station at Stromness. Astiz had agreed to this and, in the darkness, Nick had watched from the bridge of *Endurance* as a long line of torches slowly moved out of Leith, up over the hill and down the other side into Stromness. There they were met by armed Royal Marines and made to sit down on the old jetty and wait all night before being picked up, blue with cold. Next morning, without a shot being fired, Astiz surrendered. He told *Endurance* that her helicopters could fly in and land at a site prepared by the Argentinians for their own helicopters.

Before landing, the site was very carefully checked and it was found that the landing pad had been booby trapped. Had the helicopter flown straight in, it would have been blown to pieces. This incident made *Endurance* and *Plymouth* very angry and even more careful. Leith was covered in booby traps and it took the explosive experts from *Endurance* two weeks to find and defuse them all.

The Argentinian stores at Leith proved to be staggering. There were tons of drink, which the British ships were delighted to have as they were low on supplies. There was a mountain of food which was also eagerly distributed and, later on, Annie and I had a huge breakfast on board *Endurance*, consisting of Argentinian eggs, bacon and sausages. Delicious.

The gale blew for two days. The high winds came roaring in over the mountain tops and down the glaciers, slamming into the hut. While Tony and I were out walking we both had our thick, tight-fitting woolly hats torn from our heads and thrown hundreds of yards and we spent over half an hour looking for them. Pete went out to Rocky Point to check the horizon, got covered in spray from the raging and teaming sea and, at one point, had to get down on his hands and knees where the wind came funnelling through a narrow gap in the rocks that he had to pass. I watched him struggling back to the hut from the beach, going against the wind and could hardly believe it when I saw the wind physically pick him up and throw him to the ground. Pete is six feet one inch tall and weighs fourteen stone.

That evening, another message came over the radio for us: 'Positive arrangements have been made for your uplift. Stop.' I think everybody on South Georgia fell about laughing. We had been stranded on South Georgia for four weeks under Argentinian occupation. The British Navy had arrived and retaken the island. We had known for a long time that we would be picked up; in fact, we had been told over and over again that that was the case. What we wanted to know now was when this welcome 'uplift' was going to take place.

April 28th was dull but, at last, calm. Rather disappointingly, no helicopter arrived, but for the first time after a very long spell, *Endurance* made contact with us twice that day, over the radio. The first time was in the morning with a long message for me from my father: 'Three cheers – Welcome back to the fold. Everyone jubilant at spectacular naval success and all families and friends thrilled by renewed contact with St Andrew's Bay. I applied to come as guide with first craft ashore but Nott, politely and sympathetically, declined. Very disappointing.'

When I first heard this, I thought my father was joking, but on returning to England I discovered to my horror that he really had asked

Mr Nott if he could be in the first craft ashore. I have to admit that it would have been great fun if he had been, but then we weren't all down there for the fun.

'Don't burst a blood vessel, but in response to great public interest we have to network your film at 19.30 on 14 May. This includes footage brought back by me and is marvellous. Congratulations. Afterwards, we will settle down with you and produce normal super documentary.'

My father knew me very well, because I did blow a blood vessel. I could quite understand why Survival were going to make a film with the material they had received from me before all this fighting started, but by doing so, what I had hoped would be my best film yet was going to be totally changed. Now the story for the film which I had carefully constructed over the last seven months and filmed accordingly would disappear.

Good old Pa, he was obviously in cracking form and over the moon that Annie and I were safe and well. Maybe, with a bit of luck, we would be in England in time to see our film. I knew Survival would make a good job of it even if I wasn't there to help them. Later that day, *Endurance* called us all up again with the news we had all been waiting for.

'We propose to pick you up on the afternoon of Friday. Over.'

We were to be picked up first and then the other bases. Some of them had glaceriology equipment and frozen samples that had to be maintained at a temperature of minus 20 degrees. The uplift wasn't going to be as easy as it first seemed. Then we heard from the base at Bird Island that they had two ducks they wanted to take out – destined for Sir Peter Scott's bird sanctuary at Slimbridge, Gloucestershire. *Endurance* rose to the occasion and said that the ducks would be most welcome, especially when they heard they were house-trained!

I checked with *Endurance* whether my equipment, one ton in all, would be picked up by helicopter or boat. They hoped it would be by helicopter and so did I, otherwise it meant dragging a ton of heavy equipment down to the beach, and we couldn't reach the beach without crossing the Heaney melt stream. We would end up soaked and blue with cold. It would depend on the weather. Pete and Tony hoped to be flown direct to Grytviken. They needed some time there to try and find their personal equipment and also the equipment belonging to the thirteen BAS men originally taken prisoner by the Argentinians. *Endurance* thought that this was a good idea but warned Pete that the base was in a pretty bad way. There had been a lot of looting by the

Argentinians and the little post office had been broken into and nearly everything smashed.

April 29th was our last full day at St Andrew's Bay. We were sad that our time had come to leave. We had had seven wonderful months living in the little wooden hut that we had turned into a cosy home. The king penguins had proved marvellous stars and we had grown very fond of the thirty or so penguins who marched up to our hut nearly every day. The elephant seals were a constant source of amusement, even though they were ugly, smelt and had filthy habits. The albatross were gentle, graceful and beautiful. The reindeer were perhaps the most rewarding of all because when we had arrived at St Andrew's Bay on that freezing, snowy day in October, they had taken one look at us and had bolted across the snow and over the hills. Eventually, after three or four months, realising that we were not there to harm them, they started grazing right outside our hut and as long as we were slow and quiet in our movements, we were able to get to within forty feet of them.

We went to the king penguin colony to say goodbye. We sat on some rocks and watched the activity around us. The chicks were now nearly as big as the adults, their fluffy brown down thick and shining, their stomachs bulging. Most of them would survive the winter. Some of the adult penguins were slowly weaving their way out of the colony to go to sea to hunt for food for their young, while others were landing down on the beach in ones or twos, hardly able to walk, so full were they of food. Squabbles and fights broke out amongst the adults here and there and the ever-present skuas, sheathbills and giant petrels dashed in and out amongst the penguins, searching for anything edible. All was well at the colony.

On the beach we stopped every now and then to scratch the back of an elephant seal or sprinkle some damp grey sand on their backs. We looked at the glaciers surrounding the bay and remembered the first time we had had to cross them and how nervous we had been, quite convinced we would disappear down a crevasse and never be seen again. The waves pounded the shoreline and a few adult penguins followed us out of curiosity. We again played Grandmother's Footsteps with them until they got bored and broke away to find something else to do. We climbed up the steep tussock cliffs to take one last look at the albatross and their young. The young birds were standing up on their nests flapping their wings, exercising and strengthening their muscles. They had moulted almost completely their pale grey fluffy down and, although it would be a few years before their plumage looked like that of an adult albatross, they were, without doubt, very beautiful.

218

Finally we walked out to the Rocky Point to see if we could see a leopard seal. The sea was grey and cold, with a heavy swell flowing, but after ten minutes of carefully peering into thick kelp beds surrounding the rocks, we spotted the nostrils just above the surface. It was patiently waiting for an unfortunate penguin to swim by within striking range.

We were rather miserable by the time we got back to the hut. We were loath to leave this wonderful island, not knowing whether we would ever return, and yet we longed to see our families back home in England.

Endurance came on the radio that evening, to confirm that a helicopter would be flying in between three and four p.m. to collect all our equipment and us. I was relieved we wouldn't have to carry the equipment down to the beach across the melt stream.

The men were itching to get to Grytviken, hoping they would find at least some of their personal possessions still there. We'd heard from the four men at Lyell Glacier who had by now reached Grytviken that everything was scattered all over the place, much was broken or smashed and valuable items of all sorts were missing. It was all rather depressing. I felt so sorry for the men. I would have been livid if it had happened to me. Pete had slides of his two years on South Georgia at Grytviken. He never found them.

We didn't do anything special that last night. There were no messages for us from Signy Island. The BBC news told us that Stanley radio had closed down because Chile had been monitoring the programmes and passing any relevant information on to Britain. I was rather pleased that I had recorded it all. Argentina, in response to Britain's air and sea blockade of the Falklands, declared a war zone of two hundred miles round the Falklands, South Georgia and the South Sandwich Islands. I wondered briefly if this would affect the pick-up due the next day. We decided to have an early night as we knew tomorrow was going to be a very busy and tiring day, so Annie and I struggled into our polar sleeping bags for the last time.

At last came the day we'd been waiting for. At eleven a.m. Signy Island called us up on the radio with a message for me from my father: 'Hope to get everything moving quickly this end and feel sure you will all be off soon. Regards to all parties. Much love.'

Early in the morning, Pete got in touch with Grytviken again to find out the state of his room and lab. It seemed that the windows had been smashed and not a lot was left. Nothing much could be done and we set about packing up our own gear.

For the last time, my solar panel was lowered carefully down from the roof and packed into its padded case. Unopened food boxes were stowed back in the depot, plus the sledge, snow shoes, ski-sticks and rucksacks, which belonged to BAS and could cope with the long winter. The men dismantled the two tents and carefully packed them up and stored them also in the depot. Every item was cleared out of the hut, plates, saucepans, knives and forks were washed and put back. Windows were cleaned and the wooden shutters fixed to them on the outside to protect them until next summer. Rubbish was burnt and buried. Water was drained out of all containers so that they would not crack when the water froze. The last two cans of paraffin were stored inside the hut. The drum of petrol outside was tied down for the winter. The Union Jack, which we had flown defiantly whenever the weather permitted, was lowered for the last time at St Andrew's Bay and carefully rolled up and packed into my kitbag. Everything was carried one hundred yards from the hut and piled neatly to wait for the helicopter. Just before I took down the radio aerial to pack it away, Nick Barker on *Endurance* came up on the radio. 'We shall be arriving as you know to collect you and all the gear this afternoon. It will be a pleasure for us if you can stay on *Endurance* for a couple of nights.'

We had just about finished packing everything up, including the radio, and were thinking about some lunch when we heard a helicopter – it had arrived two hours early. We rushed out of the hut and welcomed Tony Ellerbeck with open arms – try kissing a pilot with his huge flying helmet on – there just isn't room. He had flown in to take Pete and Tony to Grytviken but, for once, they weren't in a major hurry, so they joined us for lunch. Tony Ellerbeck told us that *Endurance* was still at Leith, clearing up the awful mess and dismantling the mass of booby-traps laid by the Argentinians. *Endurance*'s depleted larder was being replenished with three months' supply of Argentinian eggs, vegetables, fresh meat and drink.

After our last lunch of soup and ration biscuits at St Andrew's Bay, the helicopter left for Grytviken. Myles, Annie and I stayed behind for the last few hours. Annie was quite determined, in her usual domesticated way, to leave the hut spotless with everything exactly in place. So, while Myles and I did the last few jobs of tying down the depot, Annie was on her hands and knees in the hut scrubbing the floor for the second time that day. The shuttered windows were checked, last-minute bits of rubbish burnt and, finally, with everything packed and ready for the helicopter, I closed the door of the hut for what I thought was the last time, making sure the door bolt slid home fully. Then we sat down on the door step to wait.

An hour later, we were still there. A few penguins came up from the beach and stood and stared at us for a while but there weren't the usual bits and pieces lying around outside the hut for them to investigate, so after a quarter of an hour they wandered off towards the now refrozen Heaney melt stream, one or two of them tripping over the stones as they went. For the last three or four days, the sunrays had failed to touch the hut as it was below the height of the hills and mountains which surrounded St Andrew's Bay. We were living in permanent shade. Although it was a beautiful day, the sun never touched our faces and the temperature was well below freezing. While we waited, we gradually got colder and colder stamping our feet, occasionally flapping our arms, slipping on our thick padded gloves and pulling down our woolly hats a little further. We chatted quietly to each other about the last four weeks, checking our watches every now and then and hoping the helicopter would soon turn up so that we could get going. The ton of equipment lay in a huge pile not far away, everything packed up and locked, ready for the long journey home.

At five, the three of us, almost frozen stiff with cold, suddenly came to life, as we picked up the familiar sound of a helicopter. The camouflaged Wasp helicopter from *Endurance* made a perfect landing beside the pile of equipment. Instead of starting to pack everything into the sling nets straight away, Tony Ellerbeck, his observer and two helpers got out of the machine and came and joined us by the hut. They apologised for being late, but *Endurance* had only just left Leith, and Tony wanted to wait until she was nearer to St Andrew's Bay before starting to ferry all the equipment on board. This meant another delay, so I opened the door of the hut again and the five men plus Annie and myself piled into the shuttered hut and brewed up hot cups of tea. I saw Annie look in dismay at her recently scrubbed floor as all seven of us wearing heavy boots brought in everything imaginable and ground it into her clean floor. I realised this would mean a further delay while she gave it the third and final polish.

Half an hour later, we finally got going. While Annie washed up the mugs and scrubbed the floor, I filmed the men loading all my equipment into the nets, weighing each trunk and case – the helicopter could not lift more than a few hundred pounds at a time. Tony started up his machine and skilfully hovered over the first loaded net while the two helpers hitched the net onto the large hook dangling under the belly of the machine. The first load of equipment was lifted from the ground and the helicopter, gathering height and speed, turned away from the hut and out towards the sea. *Endurance* was still out of sight, just a few miles north of us. While the helicopter was away, we got the next net ready. I helped Annie hang the tea mugs up on their hooks and, giving the hut one final check, I slid home the bolt of the door again.

I was standing by the hut filming the helicopter with another load when the sudden down-draught of the blades knocked me clean over onto my back. I did a backward flip over the wooden loo which I was determined to take home with me, and found myself staring up at the sky. Annie, giggling, helped me up as the second load of equipment disappeared. It took five or six journeys to get all my equipment to *Endurance*.

Finally it was our turn. We struggled into the bright orange all-in-one suits, clipped on our life jackets, positioned the ear-fenders and with our cameras ready to roll, jumped on board. Just before take-off, I bid St Andrew's Bay and the hut farewell and thanked God for the seven wonderful months we had been given. I asked Him to keep an eye on us during the long journey home.

It was a clear, cold evening over St Andrew's Bay with not a cloud in sight. The mountains and glaciers gleamed with fresh clean snow. The penguin colony was full, with thousands more birds scattered all along the beach. Small groups of shedding elephant seals were dotted about. Our little hut with its red depot looked very lonely as it gradually faded from our view. Reluctantly, we turned away from the bay and looked towards *Endurance* waiting for us with warmth and comfort. The helicopter circled the ship and then carefully slipped in sideways and landed on the flight deck.

13

FAREWELL TO SOUTH GEORGIA

Nick Barker was there to greet us with a big smile and a warm hug. Both Annie and I tried hard to thank Nick for all that he had done for us during the last four weeks: keeping an eye on us, rescuing us, the occasional helicopter visit and what little information he could tell us. There was so much to thank him for and so few words to choose from.

Although we were both in a celebratory mood now that it seemed we were, at last, on our way home, the black-out on the portholes reminded us that we were, in fact, at war. We had been given the guest cabin with its own sitting-room and loo, although the luxury we were both looking forward to was the sheets on the beds. We were still suffering from our long wait on the doorstep of the hut and I stood, almost in a trance, as the warm shower brought some heat again to my bones.

The cabin itself was warm and cosy and we pranced about in bra and pants, delighted with it all. Then the agonising questions – shall I wear this dress or that one? Do these shoes go with my skirt? Have you got my tights? I had almost forgotten what it was like to be a woman. The delicious smell of scent, a little make-up – what bliss! I hoped we had finally killed the reek of the penguin colony though if we hadn't, I felt the officers would all be far too gentlemanly to mention it. At last we were ready.

'You go first,' I said to Annie.

'No, no, you,' she said and I left the cabin conscious that I was crossing an invisible threshold.

Nick entertained us to drinks in his cabin and I began to think that we were going to have a very enjoyable journey back on *Endurance*, especially if every evening was like this one. We were joined for dinner by an officer from HMS *Antrim*, and though I wondered why he was on board, I didn't give the matter much thought. After dinner, we went to the Wardroom to join the officers. The evening turned out to be a very jolly one and some of the pain at leaving St Andrew's Bay began to fade.

Then Nick took me aside and told me that he would not, after all, be taking us across the Atlantic. *Endurance* was still needed in the area and it had been arranged for us to transfer to HMS *Antrim*. We would not be alone, however. On board *Antrim* was Captain Astiz, the notorious butcher who had been the commander of the Argentinian forces on South Georgia. He was being held under armed guard and would be taken as far as Ascension Island and then flown back to Argentina. The tanker *Tidespring* would also be heading north with the Argentinian prisoners on board.

Both Annie and I were bitterly disappointed that we would have to leave *Endurance*. Nick and his men had been a marvellous comfort throughout our ordeal and we would have been much happier to have remained with them. However, war is war and we were thankful enough to go to sleep safe in our snug bunks – oblivious to what was going on elsewhere.

We were up at eight, while it was still dark outside, and Nick's steward, Deacon, served us with a delicious breakfast of bacon and eggs in our day cabin. What an unbelievable luxury! Up on the bridge, we watched *Endurance* prepare the airlift of the men from Bird Island and Schlieper Bay. The north-west end of South Georgia is very different from our part. There were no high, snow-covered mountains and glaciers, only small, rounded hills covered occasionally with patches of snow. This end of the island got a lot of low-lying cloud and drizzle , but this morning, 1 May, there was a crystal clear sunrise, ideal for filming. We caught the sun as it rose behind the hills. There was a heavy swell that day and at one time the ship was pitching so heavily that the helicopters were unable to land or take-off from the flight deck and had to hover nearby until things calmed down.

Meeting the men from Bird Island and Schlieper was quite a surprise. For months they had been nothing more than voices on the radio telephone, although for the last four weeks we felt they had become very close friends indeed. We had, after all, been through a lot together. They all had long uncombed hair and stubbly chins and were wearing clothes that had seen better days. However, a hot shower, a barber and a change of clothes would make new men of them. With them came two South Georgian pintails, destined for Slimbridge. With the full

224

company on board, *Endurance* turned round and headed back to anchor in the calm waters of Grytviken harbour.

Nick was sad that we were leaving him so soon. He had hoped we would have had another night aboard as we had hardly any time to chat. However, at four p.m., *Antrim* appeared a few miles away and the Wessex flew over to take the first net load. We were sorry to be leaving *Endurance* in a mad rush, with no time to say a decent goodbye or thank you – just a wave here and a hug there and shouts of 'See you in England.' I gave Nick a big hug and thanked him for all he had done for us and promised to ring his wife as soon as I reached England. In fact, several men had given us the names and telephone numbers of their wives for when we got home. We climbed into the Wasp helicopter and flew two miles to a grey warship – the destroyer, HMS *Antrim*. The ship's doctor, Alasdair MacLean, was on the flight deck to meet us.

It was snowing again and blowing hard and the poor man was frozen stiff, even though he was so well wrapped up that I could only see his nose and eyes. I realised that all the men must be feeling the cold terribly, not having had time to get acclimatised. Alasdair was longing to take us into the ship where it was warm and dry, but I insisted on staying by the flight deck to check personally all my equipment as it came on board. It was just as well that I did as my three heavy-duty twelve-volt batteries got left behind on *Endurance* and had to be flown over later. Once I was quite sure everything was where it should be Alasdair took us to where we would be sleeping – the Admiral's Stateroom.

This sounded awfully smart to me as our footsteps echoed down miles of narrow grey steel corridors and we climbed up and down vertical ladders that I knew would present a problem when wearing a skirt. Finally, we came to a highly polished mahogany door and found ourselves in the Admiral's Day Cabin. It was vast. I later paced the room out and calculated that we could have fitted five of the St Andrew's Bay huts into it. The luxury of so much space! There was an enormous conference table with twenty chairs round it, a very attractive writing desk and chair and a sofa and two armchairs. There was also a large television set which was part of the ship's internal video system and a huge electric fire.

At one end of the room was another door leading into the cabin. There was one big bunk made up and a camp bed. There was a wardrobe, chest of drawers and mirrors and a mass of telephones and switches by the bunk bed, which Alasdair asked if I would be kind enough not to use! Leading off from the cabin was a big bathroom that actually had a bath in it, though we were asked not to use it. There was a shower attachment instead. This was going to be fun. We could have a party in the day cabin with all the BAS men. Until yesterday, it had been used as the War Room and had been covered in charts, maps and photographs of South Georgia. Electricians and cleaners were trying to get the room back to normal for us. We had two stewards to look after us and Alasdair told us the Rules of the Ship – what more could one ask for?

As we had so much space, I asked Alasdair if all my equipment could be brought in so that we could organise ourselves. So sailor after sailor trooped in, red in the face, puffing and panting, bringing in trunks, camera cases, boxes and batteries and neatly piled them up at one end of the room. I checked the electric points to make sure I could safely charge up my cameras. One thing I was determined to do was to get some film at Grytviken, in particular the *Santa Fe* and the base.

I went along to see Captain Young and asked if I could be landed at Grytviken. I could see from his face that he was reluctant to fly me in to get some footage. *Tidespring* had a lot of Argentinian prisoners on board and as the tanker was not properly heated they were anxious to get off to warmer waters. There was also the danger of mines and booby traps at the base and although the Marines were busy clearing everything up he didn't consider it suitable for ladies. I enquired if anyone at all had taken film of either the *Sante Fe*, the crashed helicopters or the Marines now at the base. It seemed no one had. I stressed that it would be unforgivable if I was not allowed ashore when I was the only person with a camera and film to show our people back home what a marvellous job had been done in retaking South Georgia. The British people needed to see it all for themselves.

Captain Young finally agreed but he could spare me only half an hour. A launch would take us to where the damaged *Santa Fe* was tied up to the old whaling station jetty and then land us at the BAS base for a short while. I knew I could not film it all in half an hour and once there I was not going to leave until I had what I wanted, which meant I would delay everyone. Never mind, I was sure that I had done far worse things than delay the Navy.

Antrim headed towards Grytviken harbour for the night. They had to go there anyway to collect Pete, Tony and Myles and the four men from Lyell Glacier hut who were still there assessing the damage for BAS at Cambridge. Annie and I showered, changed and went down to have supper with the officers of *Antrim*. It was a very pleasant evening and later we tuned in to the BBC to hear that Britain had attacked Port Stanley and Goose Green runways.

Next morning, the steward brought us tea at seven and we went up on the bridge wings to watch the dawn breaking, cold and clear. On our starboard side was Grytviken, now in permanent shade for the next four months. *Antrim*'s launch took us first to where the *Santa Fe* lay grounded, tied up to the old whaling station jetty. I looked at the gaping hole in the conning tower and thought of the unfortunate Argentinian who had been in there when the missile struck, blowing his leg clean off. Poor chap. Once I had filmed all I wanted we cruised across the bay and tied up to the jetty by the BAS base. The whole base was crawling with Royal Marines, all armed with machine-guns, dashing in and out of buildings, walking along the pathways, dismantling and clearing up the Argentinian defence barricades and setting up mortar positions.

Some of them noticed me filming and jumped up and down in front of the camera yelling 'Hello, Mum.' Others marched past with their guns slung over their shoulders, serious and determined and obviously very proud of their achievement in retaking South Georgia. Then I ran into Pete who took me round pointing out smashed windows and bullet holes for me to film. I filmed the Union Jack and the White Ensign flying proudly at the flag pole, but what I desperately wanted to film was the inside of Shackleton House.

Pete told me that I would be staggered at the awful mess left behind by the Argentinians. But was there time? For the past fifteen minutes, I had had one of *Antrim*'s officers pleading with me to stop filming and return to the launch as the Captain was eager to get going. I kept telling the poor man, 'Just one more shot, only a few minutes more.' I knew that to get to Shackleton House and walk around inside the building filming would take me over half an hour and I would probably get the officer into awful trouble. At least, I had got the most obvious things on film, so I very reluctantly followed the officer back to the launch. Before leaving, we congratulated the Marines on the wonderful job they had done and wished them a happy winter on South Georgia. I just wished we could have stayed with them and they, amidst much laughter and friendly smiles, said they wished the same thing.

Once back on board, I was told that if I climbed onto the roof of the bridge, I could just see the crashed Argentinian helicopter lying on top of a small hill. Annie and I puffed and groaned as we carried the heavy cameras, film, batteries and tripod up the vertical steel ladders to reach the bridge roof. I could see the helicopter but it was half a mile away, so I fitted my most powerful lens and got a few feet of film. While I was filming, I could feel *Antrim*'s engines starting up and could hear the massive anchor being winched in.

One last shot of the base and the old whaling station, and *Antrim* began to turn her head out to sea. We scrambled down the vertical ladder again, handing down to each other all the equipment, and quickly made our way to the flight deck at the back of the ship. As we slowly passed *Endurance* on our way out of the harbour, Annie and I and all the BAS men waved our arms above our heads saying goodbye to our guard ship. We saw several of *Endurance*'s officers and ratings out on the decks waving back at us. No one could ever persuade us that *Endurance* was not the bravest ship of them all. I quickly stepped behind my camera, already set up, and filmed her as we slid past, horns blaring and arms waving, her bright hull gleaming in the sunshine, surrounded by snow-covered mountains and glaciers pouring themselves in to the sea. What a beautiful way to remember her.

We stayed on the flight deck watching *Endurance* grow smaller and smaller until, eventually, *Antrim* turned left heading north out to sea and Grytviken harbour disappeared from view. We both stood close together, leaning against the railings. Now that we really were on our way home, I longed to get there, but I knew I had left a part of me on the island at St Andrew's Bay.

14

FROM ONE EXTREME TO THE OTHER

The South Atlantic showed us what it was capable of within two hours of our leaving South Georgia. *Antrim* began to toss like a cork from side to side and crash up and down over the massive waves. Spray shot into the air covering the bows of the ship. We spent the whole afternoon on our bunks, occasionally dozing off. We knew that if only we could get a little food into us we would feel a lot better so we made the effort to change for supper and go down to the Wardroom. The short trip from our cabin to the Wardroom was a major achievement in itself, in skirts and high heels, going up one vertical ladder and coming down another, tottering along a narrow steel corridor, being slammed from one side to the other as the ship rolled.

Monday, 3 May was still rough and stormy but we began to shed ourselves of our Antarctic clothing and dug out lighter shirts and jerseys from one of the trunks. I took all our dirty clothes down to the Chinese laundry where, I had been warned, everything would come back half size. At mid-day, we went out on deck to see the tanker *Tidespring* and HMS *Plymouth* appear a mile off our starboard side. *Plymouth* had some mail and supplies for *Antrim*, and helicopters buzzed busily between the two ships.

I discovered that Captain Astiz was in a locked cabin, under armed guard, although he was allowed out twice daily to have a walk on the deck. I made the mistake of requesting permission to film him, a mistake which I shall always regret as permission was refused. I should never have asked, of course, but simply positioned myself discreetly somewhere and got on with it. I suppose if I were a news photographer and not a wildlife one I would have filmed first and asked later. We

229

didn't even manage to see Astiz while on *Antrim* as the decks were out of bounds while he was having his walk and the three non-Argentinian scrap-metal merchants were kept in another part of the ship.

Now that I was safely on a ship heading home with all responsibility taken out of my hands, I relaxed and found I was tired, very tired. I slept long and deeply those first few days.

A day or two later, I was chatting to a group of officers about my time on South Georgia when the First Officer came to tell us that HMS *Sheffield* had been attacked. Over two hundred men had been taken off but thirty had been lost.

This horrific news had a drastic effect on the men of the *Antrim* which was a sister ship to the *Sheffield*. The crew realised it wasn't a game any more, it really was war. We also heard that another bombing raid had taken place at Stanley and a Harrier had been shot down and the pilot lost. This added fuel to the already raging fire.

Next day, an Argentinian Boeing 707 spy plane came well within firing range of *Antrim* and Captain Young signalled for permission to shoot but, to everyone's annoyance, this was not granted. All we could do was watch through our binoculars and hope a wing or two would fall off.

The weather was now becoming much warmer; the sun shone and the water was calmer. While we sat around in the pleasant sunshine chatting, a small army of men in T-shirts and shorts would come pounding down the side of the ship and without breaking off talking or reading, we would pull in our outstretched legs to let the men pass and then stretch them out again. It was a very pleasant way to go home, though this little idyll soon came to a halt.

Now that there was so much action around Stanley, it was decided that *Antrim* could not continue to take us north and must return to the Falklands to replace *Sheffield*. (She was later to be hit by two bombs.) We would transfer to the frigate *Antelope* which would take us as far as Ascension Island where we could get an RAF plane home. We packed up everything and got ready for the transfer. Coming with us would be the two ducks. We had been going along to see them every day, along with most of the ship's company who insisted on feeding them tasty tit-bits, including sticky buns. The ducks had their own special cage positioned in a quiet corner of the passageway just outside the Wardroom. One of the scientists had asked permission for a small amount of water to be run into one of the baths so that the ducks could have a daily swim and clean themselves up. Permission had been granted and the ducks spent

230

each afternoon zooming round the bath. I wonder how many warships have had live ducks in their baths?

On our last evening, I found the ship's internal magazine which featured a cartoon about Annie and myself. It shows three sailors, with the one in the middle being led away under arrest. He turns to his guards and says: 'Honest, fellas, I only wanted to see the ducks. How was I to know the lady was in the bath as well?'

The transfer by helicopter began at nine next morning with the pintails travelling in pillowcases tied round the necks of two scientists. *Antelope* was much smaller than *Antrim* but bigger than *Endurance*. Her role was the defence of convoys and her turbine engines could propel her through the seas at very high speed. Within an hour of being on board, we all agreed that *Antelope* was going to be immense fun. We were given a small two-berth cabin belonging to two junior officers who unfortunately had to find other, temporary accommodation. The bunks were at least six feet up, with drawers and a tiny desk built in underneath. It was impossible to sit up in the bunks because of the pipes overhead, so we had to crawl or slither along to get into bed. The Captain, Nick Tobin, kindly offered us the use of his bathroom. Nick was small, dark and very good-looking. He was also very hospitable and when time permitted, entertained us to drinks in his cabin.

When I came out of my cabin I noticed the door of the opposite cabin was open and, looking in, I was surprised to find Captain Astiz the occupant. He didn't look like an Argentinian at all, let alone a man with a notorious past. He was tall, fair-haired, slim, good-looking and spoke very good English, though later he was to deny he could speak any. On a couple of occasions, I happened to meet him in the narrow passageway and each time he smiled and said hello, or thanked me if I moved aside to let him pass. Once, passing his cabin, I looked in to see what he was up to. Looking up from the book he was reading, he smiled and said: 'Hello, how are you?'

I was so startled to hear him speak that I automatically said: 'Very well, thank you,' and passed along, but not before noticing that he was wearing Pete Stark's good snow boots! If only I'd got that photograph. When I got back to England, I found a photograph on the front page of two popular national dailies which, they claimed, were pictures of Astiz. Neither was of him.

While we were on board *Antelope*, there was an Action Station practice. The alarm signal screamed throughout the ship, calling everyone to their positions. The huge guns fired, sending shock waves throughout the ship and after a few minutes the awful smell of cordite

231

filled the air. All the men wore steel helmets over their anti-flash hoods, their eyes and noses being the only bits of flesh exposed. There seemed very little protection against enemy fire for the gunner who had only a thin steel shield mounted round the gun. Up at the bows, I filmed *Antelope* lifting herself high into the air and accelerate from ten knots to thirty in a few seconds. A massive wake grew higher and higher, towering over us as the propellers bit down hard into the water. It was a thrilling show of power and speed but I didn't envy those men when the practice turned to reality and death was just round the corner.

Every evening, with the weather calm and sunny, the men would do half an hour's exercise with a PT instructor and one evening I was surprised when Annie said she needed some exercise and then joined in. She dashed around, jumped up and down and kept up with the men but when it came to the press-ups, the instructor called out in a loud voice that she needn't do them as they only made ladies' breasts bigger. The men thought this was very funny but Annie felt rather humiliated.

Sunday, 9 May was a beautiful day with a light breeze blowing and everyone wore shorts and T-shirts. There was little for us to do except sit around as we glided through the sparkling blue sea. The Captain felt that because the men had been training hard to keep fit during their long sea journey, it was also important that they should relax as well, so that afternoon, we all had a marvellous time playing cricket and volleyball, ending with a clay-pigeon shoot. I hadn't fired a gun for years but I loaded up the cartridges, put on the ear defenders, yelled 'Go' and slipped the safety catch off. Nothing happened. The man with the clays couldn't hear above the noise of the propellers at the back of the ship. I managed to shoot three clays out of five. The day was beautifully rounded off by a delicious buffet in the Wardroom, followed by a showing of *The Marathon Man*. Who would have thought that we were at war and that, a few thousand miles south of us, British Harriers were bombing Stanley Airport?

The following morning, I was amazed to receive a letter which had been delivered to *Antelope* during the night. It was from the frigate HMS *Ardent* which had passed us on its way southwards during the night. On board was an old friend – his family were next-door neighbours of ours at our holiday home in Scotland. Andrew Gordon-Lennox was the First Officer on board the *Ardent* and later, when the ship was sunk, was thankfully unhurt.

We were now only two days from Ascension and could expect to fly home to England the day after we arrived there. Annie and I had been invited to stay the night with the Administrator, Bernard Pauncefort, and his wife which delighted us as it meant we could see a little of the island. That sorted out, I then had to think about my film of Grytviken and my shots of the ships. The Ministry of Defence had sent word to *Antelope* that they would like to see the film as soon as possible as it was the only recent footage anyone had of South Georgia and they were anxious to get it on television. Unfortunately, I had to say I couldn't release it as it wasn't my property but belonged to Survival and I couldn't hand it over unless instructed to do so.

From the moment I was first informed that my film was urgently and eagerly awaited by the whole British nation, I began to have nightmares – what if the film were blank? The thought of landing in England and handing over four thousand feet of film and finding it was no good was too horrific even to think about – I dreamt about it instead.

Messages began to fly between London and ourselves and then there came a puzzling telex from my father: 'We will meet you off flight with Annie's mum. Hurrah for everyone. Press conference is inevitable but please refuse any press commitments if approached.'

Annie and I read this message over several times. What could he mean about press commitments? Why should the press be after us?

Our last evening on *Antelope* was more formal than we would have liked. We were joined at dinner by three members of the International Red Cross who had come to interview Captain Astiz and the prisoners.

After dinner that evening, we thanked the young steward who had looked after us. He was a cheerful boy and at eighteen the youngest member of the ship's company. Tragically, when the *Antelope* returned to the Falklands, it was sunk and he was one of the casualties.

Annie and I left the ship the next evening for our twenty-four-hour stopover on Ascension. We were sorry to leave *Antelope*. She was a friendly ship and we had been made very welcome. Ascension is a volcanic island, humid and dusty. Waiting for us there was Bernard Pauncefoot, small, slim, in a spotless cream tropical suit, with another message from my father. The South Georgia film was to be networked the next day and we were to prepare ourselves for the media avalanche.

The first thing we heard the next morning when we awoke at the Residency was birdsong outside our windows, something we hadn't heard for eight months. It seemed to be a good start to a very important day. The Paunceforts looked after us admirably but I found it difficult to conceal my excitement and longed to go to the airport.

233

The inside of the RAF VC-10 was nothing like an ordinary passenger plane. For a start, all the seats faced backwards – for safety reasons – and the entire middle of the plane was occupied not by seats but by cargo. As soon as everything was sorted out we took off promptly at three p.m. Occasionally one of us got up to check the ducks or ease our legs and although all RAF flights are dry Annie had her ever-present bottle of brandy in her handbag and she managed to hide among the baggage a few times to have a quick gulp. While she was having one of her illicit drinks all hell broke loose and she was nearly discovered. One of the BAS men had gone to check the ducks and while opening the trap-door they had taken him by surprise and escaped. For ten minutes we were all down on our hands and knees trying to persuade them to give themselves up. Even the RAF stewards joined in clapping and quacking until eventually the delinquent ducks were cornered and gently put back in their cage. After that, Annie had to have another swig.

It was now two a.m. and we were nearly home. The Captain invited Annie and myself to join him on the flight deck for the final run-in.

'You know, Cindy,' he said, 'the two of you have figured a lot in the papers lately and they've been saying all sorts of things about you that may not be true.'

'What sort of things?' I asked cautiously.

'Well, that you were taken prisoner by the Argentinians. That you sent out desperate messages for help, even that you're still marooned on South Georgia.'

'But that's not true,' I gasped. 'None of it.'

'No good telling *me* that,' he said. 'It's the media you're going to have to face.'

I began wondering if it wouldn't have been better if we had stayed on South Georgia.

We began the gentle descent to Brize Norton. I forgot about the media and watched the lights of England gradually grow in size. I could see the street lights and the car headlights moving along the roads. I looked over at Annie and smiled at her. Not long now. Several miles ahead of us, dead centre of the nose of the plane, I picked out the long runway lights. The throttles eased back, the flaps went down and the under-carriage locked into position for landing. With the headphones on I could clearly hear air traffic control at Brize Norton guiding the pilot in. Just a few more seconds and we would be landing on English soil. As the VC-10 crossed over the threshold of the runway, the pilot closed the throttles down and we glided in onto the runway to make a perfect landing. The time was 2.20 a.m. The doors were due to open at

2.25 precisely. I gathered up my things and checked my watch again: 2.24.

The plane came to a halt and I could hear the steps being wheeled over the tarmac. As the stewardess opened the door, the whole area was flooded in a glare of lights, and flash bulbs began popping. I turned to look at the thirteen BAS men behind me and smiled at them a little nervously. I looked at Annie beside me and asked her if she was ready. She nodded. Then, straightening up, I took a deep breath, walked over to the open door and stepped out to face the blinding lights.

BIBLIOGRAPHY

K. Bertrand, 'Carcass Island, 1765–1967'. *Falkland Island Journal*, no. 2, 1968

W. R. D. McLaughlin, *Call to the South*. London, Harrap, 1962

L. Harrison Mathews, *Sea Elephant*. London, MacGibbon & Kee, 1952

Olin Sewall Pettingill, Jr, *Another Penguin Summer*. New York, Scribers, 1975

Niall Rankin, *Antarctic Isle*. London, Collins, 1951

Sir Ernest Shackleton, *South*. London, Heinemann, 1920

Bernard Stonehouse, 'The King Penguins of South Georgia'. *Nature*, vol. 178, 1956

Bernard Stonehouse, *Animals of the Antarctic*. London, Peter Lowe, 1972

Ian J. Strange, *The Falkland Islands*. Newton Abbot, David & Charles, 1981